Dumfries and Galloway

CONTENTS

ISBN 0-86309-063-X

DISCOVERY GUIDES LTD © 1989

THE AUTHOR

PATRICIA DINGWALL was born in Northern Ireland and brought up near the sea. Travelling first to school in England and later to London University where she took a degree in English, she became very familiar with the Dumfries and Galloway region. She married into a Scottish family amd, though now living in the North of England, regularly visits her son in Scotland. She has always had a lively interest in history and enjoys country pursuits.

SERIES DESIGNER AND EDITOR:
MALCOLM PARKER
ASSISTANT EDITOR:
CAROLINE HILLERY
PRINTED IN ENGLAND
PUBLISHED BY
DISCOVERY GUIDES LIMITED,
1, MARKET PLACE,
MIDDLETON IN TEESDALE
CO. DURHAM. DL12 0QG.
TELEPHONE (0833) 40638

COVER PHOTOGRAPHS
Threave Gardens (two), Burn's Statue in Dumfries, Carlingwark Loch, Old Blacksmith's Shop at Gretna Green, and Orchardton Tower. ALL PHOTOS ARE REPRODUCED WITH THE KIND PERMISSION OF THE DUMFRIES AND GALLOWAY TOURIST BOARD. (Coded D&G TB where published within the guidebook).

Discovery Guides Limited wish to thank all those persons, organisations, official bodies and their officers, for their kind assistance in the production of this publication.

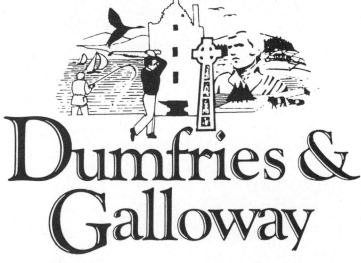

The country of Dumfries and Galloway is famous for its rich variety, with a coastline stretching from the wide sands of the Solway to the rocky cliffs of the Irish Sea, and with barren mountains and dark forests descending to green river valleys and fertile farmland. Lying, as it does, to the extreme south-west of Scotland, it is easily missed by those who travel north or south on the fast roads in the east of the region. You must turn aside to discover it - and, if you do, you will be richly rewarded.

This is a region of great natural beauty. To the east are the tidal flats of the Solway Firth, of a scale and breadth not found elsewhere in Scotland. To the west, you can stand on the cliffs of the Rhins of Galloway and gaze across to the Mull of Kintyre, the Antrim Coast and the Isle of Man. To the north are the highest mountains of Southern Scotland and the largest Forest Park in Britain. The area is divided by valleys, with unpolluted rivers flowing through the rich and green farmland which lies between the hills and the sea. Here are many small towns and villages, attractively laid out in the C18th by prosperous landowners, with spacious streets and sturdy, well-proportioned houses and cottages, where any feeling of severity is banished by their being colour-washed, cream, green, blue, pink or buff, or the white so favoured in the Rhins district. Ridings of the Marches, colourful processions, gala days and festivals add to the liveliness.

Many remains of ancient Neolithic and Bronze Age man lie scattered throughout the district, left by distant peoples who chose outstanding sites for burial cairns, left strange cup-and-ring markings on certain rocks, and were able to manipulate huge stones to make their mysterious circles. Fascinating, too, are the discoveries now being made about Whithorn, adding to our scant knowledge of the Dark Ages, when this was a centre of learning and a shrine to which many thousands of pilgrims made their way in the succeeding centuries. These later centuries saw the building of great monasteries where piety flourished, while at the same time bloody wars between Scots and English left the great defensive fortresses, and the later border strife dotted the countryside with forbidding tower houses, their menacing ruins standing today among peaceful hills and valleys. The past abounds, too, with tales of martyred Covenanters, witches and smugglers.

An immense range of outdoor activities will appeal to many, the challenging walks, the wild countryside, the opportunity to sail,

canoe or windsurf. The long Loch Ken, at the heart of the region, has been developed as a centre for water-sports of all kinds, including a section for power-boating and water-skiing, the Loch being so extensive that sailing and windsurfing can still be enjoyed without disturbance. If you prefer the sea, Loch Ryan can offer similar facilities. There are bays where you can row small boats, and little harbours from which a sailing boat can reach the Irish Sea. Yachting is growing in popularity, and ports and inlets in summer are bright with the sails of boats, while their owners enjoy the camaraderie of like-minded enthusiasts all along the coast.

The fisherman is in his element, for the rivers are full of salmon and sea-trout, while streams and lochs abound in brown trout, as well as pike and other coarse fish, and, of course, there are numerous opportunities for sea-angling, where you may catch anything from a mackerel to a shark!

If you are looking for a chance to relax and unwind, there are sandy beaches for children to play on and rocky coves to explore, and magnificent walks along cliff tops, where isolated lighthouses stand as warning beacons on the headlands. Much of the land is occupied by the Galloway Forest Park. You can picnic in a secluded grove, surrounded by the aromatic scent of pine needles on a warm day, or walk or ride through tall trees with the sunlight sending shafts of brightness amongst the shadows, or visit a wild goat park or a red deer range. Here, too, is Glentrool, a famous beauty spot, with a winding loch, rushing waterfall and trees amongst craggy hills.

For those who prefer nature tamed rather than wild, there are remarkable gardens to be enjoyed, as the mild climate of the region enables many exotic plants to be grown. There are tennis courts, bowling greens, boating ponds and parks, museums to be explored, and woollen mills and craft workshops to be visited. Dumfries and the surrounding district is closely associated with Robert Burns, who spent the last years of his life here. This is Scotland, and so there are plenty of golf courses, of both championship standard and for less serious 'holiday' rounds.

Come in autumn, and you can see the exciting arrival of thousands of barnacle geese at their wintering grounds by the Solway Firth, where special bird-watching tours are arranged. The huge variety of bird life to be seen throughout the region, both coastal and inland, is a constant delight to visitors.

It's Different

GALLOWAY
-FOREST PARK-

There is so much to see and do in this scenic area in the heart of the Highlands of South West Scotland.

Camping and Caravanning – There are two sites within the forest park which are ideal bases from which to explore the Park and surrounding countryside.

Caldons – near Loch Trool in the heart of the Galloway Hills, 14 miles north of Newton Stewart; and

Talnotry on the scenic Queens Way (A712), 7 miles east of Newton Stewart. Three sites at Borgan, Daltonae and Caldons are also available for Youth Organisations at no extra charge or for a nominal fee.

Kirroughtree Visitors Centre – It offers you a chance to experience the story behind todays living forest with walks and displays in the Exhibition Centre.

Fishing – Coarse and Trout fishing are available throughout the forest park on a day permit basis.

Wildlife – The Deer Museum at Clatteringshaws features displays on wildlife. Red Deer Range and Wild Goat Park·provide opportunities for viewing usually elusive animals close at hand. All these are situated on The Queens Way (A712) between New Galloway and Newton Stewart.

Forest Drive – Follow the historic Raiders Road along the banks of the Black Water of Dee between Bennan and Clatteringshaws with lovely picnic sites along the way. Opens 13th May till 23rd October. £1 coin machine.

Forest Walks – Make your choice from many marked trails and walks with places of historic interest to see.

Further Details – Relevant brochures and Fishing Permits can be obtained from the Forestry Commission Office, Creebridge, Newton Stewart, Wigtownshire DG8 6AJ. Tel: (0671) 2420

Outside the Forest Park – Solway Forest at Mabie, 4 miles south west of Dumfries, Fleet Forest at Gatehouse of Fleet with information centre. Forest of Ae, 10 miles east of Dumfries and also Dalbeattie Forest.

For further information contact the Forestry Commission, 55 Moffat Road, Dumfries. DG1 1NP. Tel: (0387) 69171.

TOURIST INFORMATION CENTRES

DUMFRIES TOURIST OFFICE
Whitesands,
Dumfries, DG1 2SB
Tel: (0387) 53862
This centre is open all year and has
a 24-hour answering service.

The following centres are open from Easter to
mid-October:

CASTLE DOUGLAS
Markethill
Tel: (0556) 2611

DALBEATTIE
Car Park
Tel: (0556) 610117

GATEHOUSE-OF-FLEET
Car Park
Tel: (0557) 4212

GRETNA
Annan Road
Tel: (0461) 37834

KIRKCUDBRIGHT
Harbour Square
Tel: (0557) 30494

LANGHOLM
High Street
Tel: (038 73) 80976

MOFFAT
Churchgate
Tel: (0683) 20620

NEWTON STEWART
Dashwood Square
Tel: (0671) 2431

SANQUHAR
The Tolbooth will have a centre
when restoration is complete.

STRANRAER
Port Rodie Car Park
Tel: (0776) 2595

Information is also available, for people
travelling north, at Southwick Service Station
on the M6 in Cumbria.

PUBLIC TRANSPORT
Western Scottish Omnibus Ltd.
Whitesands, Dumfries.
Tel: (0387) 53496

USEFUL INFORMATION

COUNTRYSIDE COMMISSION FOR SCOTLAND
Battleby, Redgorton,
Perth PH1 3EW
Tel: (0738) 27921

COUNTRYSIDE RANGER SERVICE
(For information about long-distance walking)
Department of Physical Planning,
Dumfries and Galloway Regional Council,
Council Buildings,
Dumfries DG1 2DD
Tel: (0387) 67611

FORESTRY COMMISSION
Head Office
231 Corstophine Road,
Edinburgh EH3 5RA
Tel: (031) 334 0303
South Scotland Conservancy
55 Moffat Road,
Dumfries DG1 1NP
Tel: (0387) 69171

NATIONAL TRUST FOR SCOTLAND
5 Charlotte Square,
Edinburgh EH2 4DU
Tel: (031) 226 5922

SCOTTISH YOUTH HOSTELS ASSOCIATION
7 Glebe Street,
Stirling FK8 2JA

There are hostels at Minnigaff,
Kendoon and Wanlockhead.

WILDFOWL TRUST
Eastpark Farm,
Caerlaverock,
Dumfriesshire DG1 4RS
Tel: (0387) 77 200

MAPS OF THE AREA
Ordnance Survey 1:250,000 Routemaster
Series
3 Western and Central Scotland
Ordnance Survey 1:50,000 Landranger Series
77 Dalmellington & New Galloway
78 Nithsdale & Annandale
79 Hawick & Eskdale
82 Stranraer & Glenluce
83 Newton Stewart & Kirkcudbright
84 Dumfries & Castle Douglas
85 Carlisle & the Solway Firth
Burns Country Official Tourist Map 1:200,000
Useful for tourists, showing historic sites,
recreational facilities and picnic places.

Geology of the Area

The shaping of the landscape of Dumfries and Galloway began more than 500 million years ago when the shifting of the earth's crust led to the closing up of a sea filled with muddy deposits. These deposits were uplifted and folded to form the great range of hills which we now call the Southern Uplands of Scotland. Since then, millions of years of erosion by water, wind and ice have reduced the hills to a fraction of their former height, exposing great masses of granite which were formerly buried deep below the surface.

Although the folded mudstones from the Ordovician and Silurian periods underlie much of Dumfries and Galloway, three large masses of granite create small areas of landscape with their own special character. These are at Dalbeattie and the neighbouring hill of Criffel, at Cairnsmore of Fleet overlooking Newton Stewart, and in the hills between Merrick and the Rhinns of Kells in the Galloway Forest.

The area seems to have remained above sea level for much of the time since then, so the ancient rocks have not been obscured by later deposits as they have further south.

However, coal deposits around Sanquhar and Thornhill in Nithsdale suggest that during the Carboniferous period, about 300 million years ago when Britain lay close to the Equator, the area may have had a cover of tropical forest. Further south, fringing the Solway Firth in places, are found deposits from this same period. Though mined in the past, the coal deposits are too small to be of any economic importance today.

The subsequent Permian period, around 250 million years ago, saw desert conditions cover the area, leading to extensive deposits of wind-blown sand stained red by oxides of iron. these New Red Sandstones, as they are called, are finely bedded, and contrast with older and coarser water-laid Old Red Sandstones of the Central Valley of Scotland. The largest deposits of the New Red Sandstone are to be found around Dumfries, Lochmaben, Moffat and Thornhill in the east, and to the south of Stranraer in the west. The soft sandstones are easily eroded, and are largely confined to the dales.

Even if the Carboniferous and Permian deposits once covered a larger area, all traces of them have been removed by subsequent erosion, exposing the older rocks beneath. Nor are there any rocks from more recent geological periods to be found in the area.

The final shaping of the Dumfries and Galloway landscape took place during, and immediately after, the ice ages which began between one and two million years ago. When the ice reached its greatest extent, the uplands were completely submerged beneath a radiating ice-sheet which smoothed and rounded the summits of the hills. Although the ice caused some minor changes to the drainage, the general character of the area, with its series of southward running dales emptying into the Solway Firth, remained unchanged. In the lowland areas along the Solway coast, and particularly on the Machars, the ice deposited considerable amounts of boulder clay, covering the underlying rocks and producing its own characteristic hummocky terrain.

Subsequent changes in the relative level of the land and sea have resulted in the creation of raised beaches, which may be seen along parts of the coast. The Solway coast is characterized by extensive deposits of mud and sand, creating areas of mud-flat and salt-marsh which are important wintering grounds for geese and wading birds. Elsewhere, more resistant rocks form stretches of cliffs and headlands. Further inland the high rainfall encourages the formation of blanket peat in areas with poor drainage. Peat cutting and afforestation have taken their toll of these deposits in recent times, however.

As you travel through Dumfries and Galloway, you will see the underlying geology reflected in the stones used for building. Thus the houses of Dumfries and Moffat, the great mansion of Drumlanrig and the larger part of Sweetheart Abbey are of sandstone, while the towns of Dalbeattie and Newton Stewart are of granite.

At one time quarrying and mineral extraction made an important contribution to the economy. The mineral rich hills to the north-east of Sanquhar contained large amounts of lead ore, and even yielded gold and silver at one time. Mining has long since ceased, but is remembered in the Lead Mining Museum at Wanlockhead.

Criffel granite from Dalbeattie proved to be suitable for harbour construction, and was easily exported by boat. It was used in Liverpool, Newport and Swansea and may even be found on the Thames embankment in London! Railways, too, allowed stone to be moved more cheaply, with the result that the banded New Red Sandstones are also widely distributed and the Locharbriggs recently quarry supplied stone for the new Burrell Museum in Glasgow.

History of the Area

From Prehistoric Man to Early Christians

On a magnificent site overlooking the sea are the huge stones of the Cairnholy Chambered Cairns, some 5000 years old. We can tell that such sites were in use over successive generations but of the social life or beliefs of the people we know little, though it must have required considerable organisation to move these huge boulders. Nor do we know much more about their successors, the Bronze Age people, except that they were, in addition, skilled metal workers. We do not know what use they made of the stone circles at Torhouskie or Holywood, nor the reason for the cup-and-ring markings on stone outcrops in the region. Theories abound, from astronomy or religous practices to metal prospecting. During the last 1000 years before Christ these distant peoples were superseded by the Iron Age Celts. With long iron swords, horses and chariots, sophisticated pottery and metal work, they swept across Europe from the Danube and became the fiercest of the tribes to oppose the Roman empire. 'War-mad, high spirited and quick for battle' was how one Roman historian described them, and the many hill forts and defended homesteads of the time bear witness to the uncertainty of life at this period. During the C1st and C2nd AD the Romans pushed north into Scotland, but they never settled in the area, leaving evidence only of the forts built to guard their route.

Galloway eventually became part of the Celtic kingdom of Rheged and probably had communities of Christians even before the arrival in the C5th of St. Ninian to become their bishop. The numerous carved stones of the Whithorn area and those of Kirkmadrine in the Rhins point to a flourishing Celtic Christian church during the so-called Dark Ages. Other influences and pressures were at work also for some stones bear evidence of Norse influence, while the great carved stone cross at Ruthwell is a monument to the Northumbrian and Roman form of worship in the C8th.

The Early Middle Ages and Robert Bruce

It was not until the C10th or C11th that Scotland became in any sense a single nation, Kenneth McAlpin being crowned King on the Stone of Scone in 843, though still only effectively controlling a small part of the country. It was still a Celtic state and the language of king, nobles and people was Gaelic. But in the C11th Malcolm III became king. He had spent many years in England and had married there, and on his return to Scotland he invited many Normans to his court, including the two de Brus brothers from Brix in Normandy. Among later arrivals were the de Balliols. These Norman lords built their usual motte and bailey castles, the Motte of Urr and Druchtag being typical examples. Successive kings, too, encouraged the foundation of abbeys under Anglo-Norman abbots, the Cistercians, who held the abbeys of Dundrennan and Glenluce being famous for their civilising influence and the development of farming on previously barren country. The border was fluid, many lords owning property in both England and Scotland. Galloway people still spoke Gaelic, the king and the nobility spoke French, monks and abbots, the literate class, used Latin, while English became more and more the language of the border region. The C12th and C13th, with capable and long-lived kings, were peaceful years which saw the building of churches and monasteries and also the emergence of towns and the founding of royal burghs.

Then in 1286 Alexander III was killed by a fall from his horse. His only heir was a three year old granddaughter, the Maid of Norway, who died on the stormy voyage from Norway. Immediately thirteen Scottish lords laid claim to the throne, among them Bruce and Balliol. Edward I of England was invited to arbitrate and he chose Balliol, expecting that Balliol would then pay homage to him as overlord. Balliol, however, arranged an alliance with France. He also confiscated the lands of Bruce, who had paid homage to Edward, and gave them to his brother-in-law Comyn. The furious Edward invaded Scotland and to make his conquest complete went on to seize the Stone of Scone, Caerlaverock surrendered to him and the Dumfries region now had to endure many years of bloodthirsty warfare. Six times Edward, 'the Hammer of the Scots', invaded the country, trying to subdue the Scots to his will.

Although Robert Bruce had paid homage to Edward, he still believed thet the crown of Scotland was his by right. Comyn was now his main rival. He offered Comyn an earldom and large estates if he would back his claim. But Comyn revealed the plan to Edward, hoping to advance his own claim. The furious Bruce, meeting him in the church at Dumfries, stabbed him. 'I doubt I have slain the Comyn,' he cried as he rushed from the church. 'Doubt!' exclaimed one of his followers, 'I'll mac siccar,' and ran into the church to finish the deed. Bruce now raised his standard and had himself crowned king, although he was almost immediately forced to retreat to the hills. But in 1307 his brilliant guerrilla tactics ambushed and slaughtered an English army in Glentrool, an event now commemorated by a stone monument. Another successful encounter is recalled by a granite boulder near the Queen's Way. Edward I died, to be succeeded by his incompetent son Edward II. By 1311 the English had been driven out of Galloway and in 1314 Bruce won the famous battle of Bannockburn. He was now undisputed king. Among his early acts were the confiscation of the lands of the Balliols and Comyns.

The Later Middle Ages

But when Robert Bruce died, his son was only five years old and in place of the incompetent Edward II, the energetic Edward III was king of England. The fierce border warfare began again. The castle at Lochmaben, a strategic point, was lost and recaptured twelve times. Other castles, however, held out, including Loch Doon, and the total conquest of the border region eventually proved too costly for Edward. Meanwhile, without the authority of a strong king, people looked to their nearest great lord for protection. And among the greatest of all were the family of Douglas. They were lords of Galloway, Douglasdale, Annandale, Clydesdale, Lothian, Stirlingshire and Moray, a power great enough to threaten the king himself. This was a time of constant struggle between the king and his nobles. In 1452 James II murdered the 8th Earl of Douglas, and three years later beseiged the Douglas stronghold of Threave Castle, bringing up the great cannon Mons Meg to batter it into surrender.

In these borderlands kinship was the basis of society and loyalty to the monarch meant less than loyalty to the clan. 'They will be Scottish when they will and English at their pleasure,' complained one official. A laird could summon the men of his clan to ride with him, and the word 'ride' was the same as 'raid', for these were raiders first and farmers a poor second. Loot, booty and cattle thieving were their main sources of wealth. Kings on both sides made efforts to check the lawlessness, dividing the Borders into a series of Marches with wardens on either side to settle disputes, but though the wardens might exact fines or demand promises, enforcing a settlement was a different matter. Large or small bands of men going by secret ways would descend on a peaceful village or hamlet, kill anyone who opposed them and drive off sheep, cattle and horses. The desolate country around the Esk was a hiding place for robbers and fugitives from justice as well as the home of the notorious Armstrongs, whose former tower house can be seen from the A7 road (but not visited). If a man was not fighting the English or engaged in a raid, he might well be fighting his neighbour, for feuds between families were constant. In this life a fortified dwelling was a necessity and a large number of tower houses remain from these turbulent times.

James IV, who succeeded in 1488 was the most popular king since Robert Bruce. He was said to have been able to leap on to a horse and ride 100 miles without stirrups. He married the English princess Margaret, the sister of King Henry VIII. He set out to encourage education, learnt Gaelic to extend his authority in the Highlands, and set up courts to deal swiftly with warring families. Then in 1512 Henry VIII attacked France. The French called on their old ally Scotland for help. James, married to Henry's sister, probably had no wish for war but he set out with 35,000 men, only to be defeated at the disastrous battle of Flodden. By the end of the day the Scottish king and most of his nobility lay dead.

Once again Scotland had a child as monarch. The Earl of Angus, a Douglas, kept the young King James V virtually a prisoner until the age of 16, when he escaped to rule for himself. His ambition was to equal the other Renaissance princes of Europe and he married Mary of Guise, with a dowry of 120,000 French livres, enabling him to spend lavishly on the royal palaces and set up a grand court. He asserted his authority over the recalcitrant nobles and tried to bring some order into the border lands by hanging Johnnie Armstrong of Gilnockie together with forty of his men. But peace with England could not be secured and James set out to meet the threat. While he himself remained at Lochmaben Castle, his army crossed the Solway, to be totally routed by a smaller English force at the battle of Solway Moss. James returned to Falkland Palace where he died three weeks later. One week before his death, news was brought to him that Mary of Guise had borne him his only heir, a daughter. 'It cam wi' a lass and it'll pass wi' a lass,' was all he could bring himself to say.

Mary Queen of Scots and John Knox

The Catholic faith was losing ground in Scotland. Few people attended church. Tithes were demanded but went to support not the parish churches but the great cathedrals and abbeys, where monks and clergy could be seen living lives of luxury. Cardinal Beaton was known to have nine illegitimate children and Bishop Hepburn eight. By the early C16th

Protestant books and pamphlets were being smuggled in from the continent where the teachings of Martin Luther and the Reformation were spreading. One of the leaders was John Knox, whose statue stands alongside that of Calvin in Geneva today.

Mary of Guise, French and Catholic, had her infant daughter crowned Queen of Scots in 1543. At the age of five Mary was sent to France and in 1558, the same year that Elizabeth became Queen of England, she married the Dauphin Francis. In the eyes of many people, and of the Catholic Church in particular, the divorce of Henry VIII and his marriage to Anne Boleyn were unlawful and Elizabeth an illegitimate child with no claim to the throne. Mary Queen of Scots now laid claim to the English throne by direct descent from her grandmother Margaret, the sister of Henry VIII and daughter of Henry VII. But by 1560 Francis was dead and Mary on her way back to Scotland, a widow of no further use to France.

In 1559 Knox had preached in Perth, denouncing the Roman Catholic Church as idolatry and causing a riot which led to the destruction of abbeys and monasteries. By 1560 the Estates (the Scottish Parliament) had abolished the authority of the Pope and forbidden the celebration of mass. Protestantism was now triumphant in Scotland. There were to be no more bishops, but superintendants to take over their districts. Responsibility in religious matters would be shared by laymen, to be known as Elders of the Kirk, and ministers were instructed to speak in Scots, not Latin, while everybody was to read and understand the Bible. Nobody was to kneel and all idolatrous relics were to be thrown out of churches. To this kingdom Catholic Mary returned. Knox fulminated against her attendance at mass and against the pagan rites of dancing enjoyed in her court, but, at first, Mary was circumspect and her marriage to the Earl of Darnley, however unsatisfactory, produced a son, James, heir to the throne of Scotland and, as long as Elizabeth remained unmarried and childless, to that of England as well. It was not her Catholic faith but the murder of her husband, followed by Mary's almost immediate marriage to the Earl of Bothwell, believed by many to have had a hand in the crime, which turned many people against her, even amongst her previous supporters. Finally defeated at Langside, Mary fled to Dundrennan. There she spent her last night on Scottish soil, crossing the Solway by boat the following day to seek help from Elizabeth, her former rival. She was to spend the rest of her life in prison in England.

The Covenanters

In Scotland, James, aged 13 months, was declared King. The Protestant nobles were determined that the king should be educated in their way. James, committed to the care of stern Presbyterians, received a gruelling education in academic subjects and had to learn by heart long passages from the Bible, starting each day with prayers, and being repeatedly told that kings derive their power from the people, and that he himself was only a subject in Christ's kingdom, the Kirk.

Elizabeth died in March 1603. Wasting no time, James set out for London. At last he was free. James enjoyed being king of England. He also admired the Church of England with its orderly heirarchy and respect for the monarchy. ' A Scottish Presbytery agreeth as well with a monarch as God and the devil, 'he once said. He determined to re-impose the rule of Bishops in Scotland and when the ministers refused to accept the change, banned the General Assembly. His son Charles I, firmly believing that kings ruled by divine right, and himself a lover of elaborate ritual in worship, had little understanding of Scotland when he abolished the presbyteries, composed of ministers and elders, and tried to introduce a new Prayer Book. In 1638 opposition to him crystallised as Scotsmen joined together in signing the National Covenant, a word taken from the Bible, 'Let us join ourselves to the Lord in a perpetual Covenant'. Charles attempted to impose his authority by force but the Covenanters had experienced soldiers in their ranks and, as general, Alexander Leslie who had been a field-marshal in the Swedish army. The king's troops were defeated and Charles forced to accept Covenant rule in Scotland. In England, meanwhile, his autocratic rule and his persecution of the Puritans had united Parliament against him, and when the Civil War started the English made common cause with the Scots by signing the Solemn League and Covenant. It was to a Scottish army under Leslie that Charles surrendered in 1643.

Charles II, after his restoration in 1660, never visited Scotland but appointed the Earl of Lauderdale as Secretary of State. All legislation passed by the Covenanters since 1633 was cancelled and ministers were instructed once more to receive their charges from bishops. Rather than submit to these orders, ministers preached in the open air at illegal conventicles, sometimes attended by thousands of the faithful, and often in the hills or remote places.

John Graham of Claverhouse, Viscount Dundee, 'Bonnie Dundee' to his Highlanders but 'Bloody Clacers' to the people of Dumfries and Galloway, together with his hated henchman Sir Robert Grierson of Lag pursued the Covenanters with unparalleled ferocity, executions and tortures, which included rolling some downhill in spiked barrels and drowning two women by tying them to a stake in the rising tide. Memorials to slaughtered Covenanters abound in the region and this period has come to be known as 'The Killing Times'. In 1680, as a gesture of defiance, Richard Cameron declared war on Charles II as tyrant and usurper at Sanquhar. Cameron was quickly trapped and killed, but his cause was taken up by Donald Cargill and when he,too, was caught and executed, by James Renwick, also martyred, whose monument stands close to Moniave. He was the last of the Covenanters to be executed, for the persecution ended when the Protestant William of Orange became king and Scotland once more became presbyterian, with the government of the Kirk restored to the elders and ministers.

C18th Prosperity and C19th Expansion

By the end of the C17th people were exhausted by years of conflict. In 1706 the Scots acquiesced in the Union of the two parliaments and accepted the accession of the Hanoverian George I in 1714. The two attempts, in 1717 and 1745, to restore the Stuart kings met with little support in the Lowlands. Bonnie Prince Charlie passed through Dumfries on his retreat from England but his ill-dressed and, in the eyes of the local people, semi-barbaric gaelic-speaking Highlanders found little sympsthy. There were some sunsequent benefits, however, in the improvement of roads, designed to ensure more rapid troop movement, if needed in the future, and a better road now traversed the region all the way to Portpatrick.

As Scotland was opened up, opportunities for trade increased. The first 'improvers' of agricultural land were the landlords of Dumfries and Galloway, with new methods of liming and manuring and the careful breeding of better stock. Dumfries became the centre of a vast cattle trade, where cattle were collected from all over the region, and even from the Highlands and Islands, to be sent to the farmlands of the North and East of England to be fattened before being sent on to feed the growing industrial towns. Before the days of trains, they had to travel by foot and herds of 40 or 50 would be put into the charge of a drover to travel by recognised 'drove roads' which avoided towns and cultivated areas to great cattle fairs in England. The mileage to Huntingdon, one centre of cattle trading, is still recorded on the Midsteeple in Dumfries.The great landlords could now build themselves grand mansions such as Galloway House or Arbigland, and set about improving their grounds by planting trees and gardens which still give pleasure to many visitors. Villages and towns were laid out to new and improved plans and many elegant town halls date from this period. Attempts to establish a cotton textile industry were less successful than the woollen industry, where the raw material was to be had locally and where there was already a tradition of hand weaving and knitting. The lead mining at Wanlockhead was developed and expanded and the quarrying of sandstone and granite added to the wealth of the area.

By the beginning of the C19th, turnpike roads, funded by tolls, added to the ease of movement. Thomas Telford, the great engineer, had been born at remote Westerkirk in Eskdale and started his career as an assistant bridge builder in Langholm. The bridge over the Dee at Tongland, was built to his design and opened in 1807. Another famous road builder, John MacAdam, was born at Carsphairn. It was a time, too, of new ideas and invention. In 1788 a steamboat had been tried out on Dalswinton Lake, and the world's first bicycle was invented by Kirkpatrick Macmillan at Keir Mill. The coming of the railway in the mid C19th enabled the area to be further developed. The Caledonian Railway ran through Gretna and Lockerbie to Glasgow, while the Glasgow and Western went by Annan and Dumfries, where the fine red sandstone stations still survive. Industrial expansion, however, was not without its cost. Until 1799 coal miners at Sanquhar were little better than slaves, bound to the collieries for life. Lead mining was hard and dangerous. The dwellings of the workers in the towns were grossly overcrowded and Dumfries suffered several epidemics of cholera, the mound in St. Michael's Churchyard being the burial place of 350 victims out of 550 who died in 1832.

Sir Walter Scotts romantic tales of Border life and Queen Victoria's devotion to the Highlands encouraged many tourists to seek out Scotland, visits now made easy by rail. Shooting, fishing and stalking became immensely popular, while the coast around Rockcliffe and Kippford were thought of as 'the Scottish Riviera', and Moffat flourished as a spa town. Great houses like Lochinch Castle, Threave and Craigcleugh were built in the newly fashionable 'Scottish Baronial' style.

In 1747, at Arbigland, a son was born to the gardener, who lived in a modest cottage on the estate. At the age of 13 the boy, John Paul, joined a merchant ship and by the age of 21 had risen to be captain of a Dumfries trading vessel. Then, possibly after killing a man in a brawl, he suddenly abandoned the service and went to America. Here he added the name of Jones to John Paul. When war broke out between America and England, John Paul Jones, an experienced sailor, was given command of an American ship and set out to raid the British coast, his previous knowledge of the Solway being most useful to him. His most renowned exploit was in 1779 when he defeated a British frigate off Flamborough Head in the North Sea. As Jones's ship seemed about to sink, the British captain called on him to surrender. 'I have not yet begun to fight,' was Jones's famous reply, before going on to win the engagement. He later assisted the Russian navy and also spent much time in France, where he was a great success and immensely popular with the ladies. Regarded as 'father of the United States Navy', a plaque to his memory has been put on the cottage at Arbigland.

One of the greatest engineers of all time, Thomas Telford, was born in Eskdale. His widowed mother earned only a scanty living and the boy soon learnt to make himself useful herding cattle or helping on farms. Always cheerful, he became known as 'laughing Tam'. About the age of 15 he was apprenticed to a stone-mason in Langholm, where the Duke of Buccleuch was improving the houses of his tenantry. Telford's industry, intelligence and love of reading interested a kindly Langholm lady, who let him use her small library, where he developed a lifelong love of literature. A long poem by him, 'Eskdale', a celebration of his native district, was published in 1784. In 1780 Telford had moved to Edinburgh and he later went on to a famous career in England and Wales as well as in his native Scotland, where he built roads, bridges, harbours, and the Caledonian canal. The bridge at Tongland is one of more than 1,200 bridges designed by Telford. Laughing Tam grew up into a man described by all his contemporaries as 'heartily to be liked', 'universally acquainted', 'of infinite humour and a strong enterprising mind'.

Hobby horses, a bar and saddle positioned above two wheels and pushed along the ground by the rider's feet had been in use since the late C18th, but it was Kirkpatrick Macmillan, a blacksmith's son in Keir, who first thought of attaching treadles with connecting rods working on the rear axle. On this primitive first bicycle Macmillan rode 60 miles to Glasgow, to prove that his invention worked. There people crowding round to see this unusual machine caused such confusion that Macmillan was hauled before the magistrate and fined five pounds. On seeing the bicycle, however, the magistrate was so impressed that he refunded the fine out of his own pocket. Macmillan, who became known as 'Mad Pate' and the 'Devil on Wheels', was more interested in inventions than money for he allowed anybody to copy his idea.

Robert Burns is given a separate chapter in this guidebook. Another famous writer, Sir Walter Scott, often visited the district and had a friend, Joseph Train, an excise man in Newton Stewart, who sent him stories, anecdotes and even antiquities. Scott's 'Old Mortality' was based on Robert Paterson, a stone-mason who cut the tombstones of Covenanters, and Jeanie Deans, in 'Heart of Midlothian' was drawn from Helen Walker of Irongray, where her gravestone was erected by Scott, while the smuggling background of 'Guy Mannering' is set near Dumfries. 'Two Drovers' is a remarkable account of the men who drove cattle from Scotland to the English markets.

Other literary figures include Carlyle, born at Ecclefechan, and J.M. Barrie who was at school in Dumfries and who wrote 'Bandalero the Bandit' for the Dumfries Amateur Dramatic Club. Richard Hannay is pursued around Cairnsmore of Fleet in John Buchan's 'The Thirty-nine Steps', and Dorothy Sayers' 'Five Red Herrings' can be followed from Kirkcudbright. A bronze otter near Monreith is a memorial to the naturalist Gavin Maxwell, famous for his 'Ring of Bright Water'. His book 'The House of Elrig' describes his childhood in this region, where he was born (Drive number 4 takes you past Monreith and close to Elrig). A remarkable monument to Hugh MacDiarmuid, the Scottish poet, stands on a hillside outside Langholm. The eye-catching obelisk on the top of Duncraig Hill near A712 commemorates Alexander Murray (1775-1813) a shepherd's son who, not strong enough for outdoor work, taught himself so brilliantly that he became the finest linguist of his day, his knowledge extending even to languages like Phoenician, Chinese and Sanskrit. The minister at Urr, he was much loved and 3,000 people were at the laying of the foundation stone in 1834. Nearby 'The Raiders Road' is named after a work by S.R. Crockett (1860-1914) an immensely popular novelist, born at Laurieston. Artists who have chosen to live here have included E.A. Hornel, whose former home can be visited in Kirkcudbright.

The Coastline

Stretching from the Solway Firth to Loch Ryan are over 200 miles of varied coastline, headlands, rocks, shingle, sands and mudflats. The cliffs of the Rhins of Galloway take the full force of the Irish Sea and the rest of the coast is a series of rocky headlands, with sand and shingle washed into the sheltered bays between them. All round the coast are numerous creeks, inlets and small harbours, all used in past days for legitimate or nefarious but profitable trade. The large rivers of the Nith, the Urr, the Dee, the Cree and the Annan, the Water of Fleet and the Water of Luce flow through wide sandy estuaries, while the Esk, though actually entering through England, has created the sands and salt marshes of the Solway Firth, a paradise for birds.

Until the building of good roads in the C18th, travel by land was difficult and the transport of goods slow and laborious. Travel by water was usually easier. Even after the roads had been improved, it was not until the coming of the railways in the C19th that the overland carriage of heavy goods, such as coal or stone, became simple. Although harbours were not suitable for the largest ships, two masted vessels , brigs, schooners, ketches and sloops sailed in and out of the ports, while luggers and small boats with oars could use the innumerable creeks and sandy beaches. The rivers upstream as far as Dalbeattie and Dumfries were navigable for medium sized boats, and the quays at Kingholm and Glencaple were familiar to Burns in his work as an excise officer. Places such as Creetown, Wigtown, Portpatrick, Port William, Port Logan were in use for regular commerce, as well as Stranraer and Kirkcudbright, both much used today. Heavy goods, lime and coal came in to Sandhead, while granite from Dalbeattie was shipped out in huge amounts. The jetty at Port Logan was built out in a wide sweep to enclose the bay and improve this exposed harbour for the landing of vast numbers of Irish cattle.

Portpatrick had long been a main crossing point to Donaghadee on the other side of the Irish Sea, and a regular packet boat postal service had operated between the two ports as early as l662. Portpatrick also became the 'Gretna Green' for Ireland (where the same laws about parental consent applied as in England) and many lovers made their hasty marriages there. By the mid C19th, however, steam packets were operating and Stranraer, with its much more sheltered harbour, increased its trade while Portpatrick's declined. The official Irish ferry service started from Stranraer in l862.

Sailing these exposed waters, however, was never simple. The exposed Galloway ports could be battered by storms, while fierce tidal currents ran round the cliffs of the Mull. In the Solway the tides raced in over the sands, shifting the channels and depositing new beds of silt, while many smaller harbours would dry out at low tide. Even today there are few deep water moorings for the yachts which now use them and a knowledge of weather, wind and tide is always essential. Wigtown, once a busy port and the capital of the region, was engulfed by sand in the early years of this century, and the spot where the martyrs drowned is no longer seashore but salt-marsh. The people of Dumfries made strenuous efforts to keep the port open for larger ships and in 1811 the Nith's channel was straightened, deepened and embanked. But within 25 years it needed more work done on it. The coming of the railway in l850 led to the port's eventual decline.

It was the Dumfries merchants who ordered the building of the Southerness lighthouse, one of the oldest in Scotland, in 1749, replacing an earlier beacon, to guide ships into the channel and away from the treacherous sands which here stretch well out to sea. Other lighthouses were built around the coast. That at Corsewall, to assist ships making for the Clyde, was built about 1815. It is still permanently manned   and may be visited in the afternoon, if the lightkeeper is not otherwise engaged. The sturdy little lighthouse at Port Logan dates from 1818 and that on the Mull of Galloway, 60ft (18m) high and 269ft (81 1/2 m) above sea level, from l828. The lighthouse at Killantringan, which is permanently manned and can be visited if convenient for the lightkeeper, dates from 1900 when it replaced an older one at Portpatrick. Even if the inside of a lighthouse can not be visited, a trip to it may well be worthwhile for they always, by their nature, have a spectacular setting and good views.

All along the coast ship-building and similar trades flourished. Kippford, for instance, now a holiday resort busy with yachts, once built two-masted schooners for Cumbria as well as for the local area. Then, as now, fishing provided some people with a livelihood and today visitors to Portpatrick in an evening may well see boats coming in after a day's fishing, while larger trawlers use Kirkcudbright. There are many opportunities for visitors to enjoy sea-angling - you might even catch a tope, a small shark but still a big fish, or enjoy the excitement of children if a shoal of mackerel comes into the bay. Before the days of modern ice-making plants there was no way of preserving fresh fish, and keeping fish (or fish farms) in ponds dates back many centuries. A salt water tidal fish pond, however, is remarkable and that at Port Logan has been a tourist attraction ever since it was completed in 1800 as a fresh fish larder for Logan House. The cod in it become so tame that you can feed them by hand and stroke their heads. The Solway Coast with its estuaries and mud flats, however, is home to many sea-creatures besides deep water fish, and lobsters, shrimps, cockles, mussels and even oysters were harvested in the past. One traditional way of catching flounders, or flat fish, was by paddling, with a long pronged 'leister' in a tidal creek. Just try keeping your foot down when a fish suddenly wriggles under it! Today Palnackie is the home of the World Flounder Tramping championship each year.

The rivers of the area are famed for their salmon. Salmon are spawned in rivers but spend much of their lives in the sea, returning to the rivers to spawn in their turn. Some fishermen have licences to net them at certain seasons in the estuaries, using net walls of up to 100 metres in length stretched on poles across the run of the tide, with local knowledge of the pools and channels where the fish travel. These stake nets are common, but a more unusual and traditional method is by 'haaf' nets, held by up to eight or nine men standing in line and working their net up to their chests in the running tide.

Commerce, boat building and fishing may have occupied some people, but it has been estimated that in the C18th almost the entire population was busily engaged in smuggling. Brandy, wines and spirits have always been heavily taxed and so at that time were tobacco, lace and salt. The latter hardly seems a luxury item but in the days before refrigeration was an absolute essential for preserving meat, fish and other foods for the lean winter months, and so a useful source of revenue for the government. The Isle of Man, little more than 20 miles away, was not subject to English laws, while there were excellent markets for duty-free goods in Edinburgh and the towns of the Clyde valley. Vessels might be small sailing boats with a crew of three or four men but were often enough large luggers with crews of fifty and well armed with guns. The signal that the coast was clear might be a flash of a lantern, but might equally well be an apparently innocent man trying to light a difficult pipe, or a sudden shower of sparks from the local blacksmith's forge. Names along the coast like Frenchman's rock, Dirk

Hatteraick's Cave or Manxman's Lake still recall these days. The cutters of the excise officers who tried to catch them were often slower than the boats of the smugglers, and their officers less good seamen. Amounts of contraband which they did discover were sometimes astonishing. One Wigtownshire farm had 200 bales of tobacco, 80 chests of tea and 1200 gallons of brandy. Strings of twenty or so ponies might pass quietly through the night but smugglers were also capable of defying the excise with a train of a couple of hundred, accompanied by well-armed 'lingtowmen' too strong for the revenue men to intercept. Everybody profited, from the smugglers themselves to the passer-by who might be rewarded with a bottle of brandy for a blind eye. When seven men were rebuked by the Elders of the Kirk in 1741, their crime was not that they had been smuggling , but that they had been doing it on the Sabbath day. Reduced taxes in 1806 made smuggling less profitable, and faster revenue boats and an increased military presence eventually put an end to the trade.

Travellers had journeyed through the region on their way to Ireland and a few had stopped to explore but the first real tourists and holiday-makers came with the railways. People in the Victorian era were firmly convinced of the benefits of sea-bathing, and a number of Victorian villas were built in the Rockcliffe and Sandyhills area. Indeed, the rocky coastline, cliff scenery, bays and inlets of the Colvend coast became known as 'the Scottish Riviera', and a splendid Edwardian hotel was built at Portpatrick. These places have remained favourites with tourists today, the villas joined by modern bungalows and chalets, while the small harbours are bright with the sails of visiting yachts. Past ages have left a legacy of delightful villages, clustered by a waterfront or in a crescent round a bay, their houses painted in varying pastel shades, with brightly coloured boats rocking gently in the water. So exceptional is the coastline that three areas, around the estuaries of the Nith, the Urr and the Water of Fleet, have been declared National Scenic Areas, while the National Trust for Scotland now owns several properties along the beautiful Colvend coast.

The Solway Coast Heritage Trail, signposted by a drawing of an ancient Christian cross, leads the visitor along a route past spectacular scenery, sandy beaches, colourful villages, gardens and ancient monuments. Other visitors may prefer lazing on a beach, sailing or sea-angling, or even take a day trip to Ireland.

Woods and Forests

Woodland and forest are so much a part of the Dumfries and Galloway landscape today that it is difficult to imagine that this has not always been the case. In common with much of the rest of Scotland, however, centuries of grazing and exploitation had virtually wiped out the original natural forest cover by the C17th and C8th. Private and later public afforestation has reversed this process, to the extent that forest now covers almost a quarter of the land area.

The few surviving fragments of semi-natural woodland, together with evidence preserved in the peaty soils, show that long ago south-west Scotland was largely covered with mixed broad-leaved woodland - oak, ash, birch, alder together with some Scots pine. Today's forests are mostly coniferous, made up of species which have been introduced to Britain since the C18th. In particular, Sitka spruce from the west coast of North America thrives here in the acid peaty soils of the upland areas.

Before the First World War the areas of forest were mostly associated with the great houses, and landowners who took an interest in trees. Until the C17th landowners had been more interested in the defensive advantages of their homes than in beautifying their surroundings. But by the C18th grand mansions were being constructed and the owners began to demand worthy settings for their new homes. One of the foremost among them was the 7th Earl of Galloway, keenly interested in arboriculture and silviculture, who in the late C18th devoted much time and money to the improvement of the policies round Galloway House. 'His Lordship's designs are great. He is accomplishing them by planting at the rate of 200,000 trees every year,' one visitor reported, finding to his surprise that 'every species of them thrive as well about Galloway House as in any part of England'. Although the gardens have since been redesigned, magnificent trees remain a feature of the area. Besides planting to enhance the surroundings of their mansions, landowners soon appreciated the economic value of trees, at a time when many new conifers were being introduced from the North American continent. Two of the great collectors, David Douglas and Archibald Menzies, who introduced the Sitka spruce, were, of course, Scots. Estate forestry is still important, with fine plantations to be seen at Drumlanrig, Arbigland, Castle Kennedy and Ardwell, mostly close to the Solway coast.

Extensive afforestation of the uplands to the north began after the First World War, when the Forestry Commission was established, to reduce Britain's dependence on the import of timber. Extensive planting which began in the 1920's and 1930's has been maintained since, especially in the 1960's and early 1970's, so that the Forestry Commission is now the major landowner in the area.

Early afforestation often took place with little thought for anything other than the economic return from the trees, and many plantations of the time did little to enhance the landscape. The potential of these new forests for recreation was soon perceived, however, and in 1943 Scotland's second Forest Park was established in Galloway. The Galloway Forest Park - Britain's largest - covers almost 250 square miles, though areas of upland remain unplanted. Most of this area, and a number of other Forestry Commission forests further east, are accessible to the public, and offer a range of facilities for visitors. Away from the busy Solway coast holiday areas, the forests are a haven of peace and tranquillity, to be explored at leisure.

It is possible to spend a holiday at one of two camp sites in the Galloway Forest Park, both of which have facilities for disabled holiday-makers. Forests are by no means all serried ranks of trees, and many trails can be followed through magnificent countryside, some suitable for the long-distance walker, others easily encompassed in an afternoon's stroll. Whether you are setting out with a particular objective in mind, or whether you are just exploring, there are plenty of off-the-road parking areas, at viewpoints, at the start of forest trails, or next to special picnic areas.

GLENTROOL FOREST makes up the western part of the Galloway Forest Park. At its heart is the picturesque Loch Trool winding among the hills - indeed, the old Gaelic name 'loch t-sruthail' means 'river-shaped loch'. Within the forest boundary are many areas which cannot be planted, including The Merrick which at 843m (2766ft) is the highest point in the Southern Uplands of Scotland. Such areas of open land make an important contribution to the scenic character of the area.

Not all of the forest is coniferous. Mixed woodland fringes the loch in places, and at Glenhead there survives a fragment of the original forest cover, oak with a mixture of alder, birch and hazel. Though managed and exploited in the past for tan-bark and charcoal, the wood contains much of its original flora, and is now a Site of Special Scientific Interest.

The **LOCH TROOL FOREST TRAIL** encircles the loch and may be followed from either direction. A good starting point is **BRUCE'S STONE** on the north side. At the lower end of Loch Trool are the **STROAN BRIDGE FOREST TRAILS**, with a choice of four routes of different length.

KIRROUGHTREE FOREST and **CLATTERINGSHAWS** make up much of the southern part of the Forest Park. There are many points of interest close to the A712 **QUEEN'S WAY** which runs through the area from Newton Stewart toward New Galloway. The Queen's Way was so named in 1977, to mark the occasion of the Queen's Silver Jubilee.

Close to Newton Stewart is the **KIRROUGHTREE VISITOR CENTRE**. Displays in the centre tell the story of the forest, and explain the work of today's foresters and the uses to which the timber is put. They also consider the way in which modern forestry seeks to find the balance between efficiency and the need to conserve the natural environment. From the centre you can follow the **PAPY HA BIRD TRAIL** through a variety of woodland habitats, or choose one of the four **KIRROUGHTREE FOREST TRAILS** which explore the surrounding forest. Added interest comes from the remains of lead mining activity surrounding Bruntis Lochs. Another trail takes you through **KIRROUGHTREE FOREST GARDEN**. Begun in 1956 in Stronord Wood, and inspired by District Officer John McNab, this arboretum now contains some 60 different tree species from around the world. There is a useful guide book.

In the eastern corner of the Forest Park is the **RAIDERS' ROAD FOREST DRIVE**, following an old cattle smuggling route along the banks of the Black Water of Dee. There is a toll on the road, which is open from late May to September. Parking is provided at intervals along this scenic route.

All the above trails are found in the Galloway Forest Park and are featured in greater detail elsewhere in this guide.

Other points of interest on the Queen's Way include the **WILD GOAT PARK**, the **RED DEER RANGE** and the **GALLOWAY DEER MUSEUM**. These are described in the section on Natural History.

Beyond the southern boundary of the Galloway Forest Park, at Gatehouse-of-Fleet, is the Forestry Commission's **MURRAY FOREST CENTRE**, and the associated **FLEET OAKWOODS INTERPRETIVE TRAIL**. This is an area of former estate woodland, its mature broad-leaved trees giving it a quite different character from the young coniferous plantations to the north. The trail illustrates a variety of management techniques, and includes a forest nursery which provides many of the trees planted in the district.

South of Dalbeattie on the A710 coast road are the **PLANTAIN FOREST WALKS** where there is a choice of way-marked routes. Dalbeattie Forest was among the first areas to be planted by the Forestry Commission, and it dates from 1923.

To the north of the A701 between Dumfries and Moffat is the **FOREST OF AE** (pronounced like the letter A). Planting began here in 1927, and this forest, which is mostly of spruce, now covers nearly 25 square miles. The forest village of Ae was established in 1947, to provide housing for forest workers. Three forest walks start from a picnic site about 3.22km (2 miles) north of the village.

In the eastern extremity of the area are the forests of **CASTLE O'ER** and **ESKDALEMUIR**, on the B723 and B709, north of Langholm and Lockerbie. These forests, some privately planted, are still young and will take some years to mature.

Other forest walks will be found at **MABIE**, south of Dumfries, just off the A710 coast road. A number of private estates, too, have established woodland walks, as at **DRUMLANRIG** near Thornhill. The **HODDOM ESTATE** off B725 west of Ecclefechan has a visitors' lodge to illustrate the running of the estate, and its wildlife, and has forest trails and way-marked walks among plantations of oak and beech as well as conifers.

Forestry now makes a major contribution to the economy, making productive use of marginal land and providing employment, whether in the forests themselves or in associated industries. The softwood from the area goes for sawn timber, for chipboard, and to a lesser extent for paper pulp. Re-afforestation has not been without its opponents. There are many who lament the loss of the old landscape of open hills and upland grazings. Others would say that, properly done, forestry can create new and attractive landscapes. Much effort is now being made to reconcile the sometimes conflicting objectives of economic forestry, conservation and recreation.

Farming

Cows, cattle and sheep in the fields show the importance of livestock as the mainstay of farming in this prosperous region. A few crops such as early potatoes are grown in the mild climate and there is some barley, but most farms have cattle or sheep or both. Pigs, which used to be everywhere in the past, are seldom seen and few people now have hens or ducks, once favourites of the farmer's wife. Visitors who follow the drives in this guide will appreciate the great variety of soils, rich pasture, poor grazing and moorland, all within a few miles. There are few of the small traditional farms of the past. In this competitive world farming is big business, as people will see who follow the drive through the Rhins past huge farmsteads and great modern barns. Many fields are bounded with stone walls, some of them being the traditional 'Galloway dyke' with the top stones set at wide intervals, giving an uncertain appearance which deters stock from jumping them.

Since the middle of the last century the lush pastures and a mild climate have encouraged many farmers to concentrate on dairy farming. The traditional cow used to be the brown and cream Ayrshire, bred originally in the neighbouring county, a hardy breed with milk rich in butter-fat, but in more recent years it has been displaced by the highly productive Friesian. The milk goes to large creameries which produce a variety of dairy foods. Until the C19th, however, it was beef and not dairying that was important and vast numbers of store cattle were sent to England to be fattened for the growing industrial towns. Crosses with different breeds and continental stock are popular today but the traditional galloway is still in demand, a heavily built, usually black animal with a thick coat able to shrug off wet weather and very tough and hardy, living well off poor ground unsuitable for milking cows. Most picturesque are the belted galloways with a wide white band round the middle.

In Eskdale, upper Annandale and the Glenkens, sheep predominate. The statue of the ram above the fountain in Moffat symbolizes the region's importance in the sheep and wool trade while Langholm is today the centre of a thriving wool and cloth producing area. The Blackface, a famous hill sheep breed, active and sure -footed, with long rather coarse wool, can withstand the winter weather out of doors and find a living off moorland with little extra feeding. Another famous hill sheep is the Cheviot, originating in the Borders, white-faced and without horns, prized for its good fleece of short thick wool.

The district has also been famous for its horses. Inded, 'galloway' has become a recognised word for a small hardy horse, originally produced here and supposed to have been interbred with Spanish horses which swam ashore from the wrecks of the Armada. This became the universal pack-horse for transporting goods before the advent of the railways. No less famous are the great Clydesdale draught horses, coming originally from the neighbouring district, the most obedient and gentle of animals.

The following places are open to visitors in the season. Tours have to fit in with the everyday life of the farm.

BLOWPLAIN OPEN FARM Near Balmaclellan, on A712 from New Galloway to Dumfries. Hill farm with cattle, sheep and poultry, also pheasants and peacocks, pets' corner. Tour starts at 2pm and lasts about 2 hours. Closed Saturday.

BORDER COLLIE AND SHEPHERD CENTRE On A701 between Moffat and Broughton. Once the smallest school in Scotland and now housing an exhibition about shepherds, sheep and dogs. There are several sheep-dog handling demonstrations each day. Open daily.

GALLOWAY FARM HERITAGE CENTRE A712 from New Galloway to Newton Stewart. Clydesdale horses working with C18th equipment, display of old implements and information about the farming past. Rides on carts and Clydesdales. Open from July. Closed Saturday.

LOW KIRKBRIDE FARM WALK A76, N of Dumfries. Dairy farm with cows, sheep and other stock, including belted galloway cow and calf, drystone dyke demonstration, milking, pony rides. Open daily.

PALGOWAN OPEN FARM N of Newton Stewart, beyond Glentrool village on road to Straiton. Hill cattle, sheep, sheep-dogs, stone dyking, horn craft, wool and sheep-skins. Suitable for wheel chairs. Tour starts at 2pm and lasts about 2 hours (under cover if wet). Closed weekends.

ROBGILL TOWER CLYDESDALE HORSE CENTRE Kirtlebridge, A74 between Gretna Green and Lockerbie. The home of the 'Bandirran Clydesdales', seen in the stables and in fields with their foals. Old horse drawn implements on display, photographs and video. Open at weekends only.

The Moffat Ram (D&G TB)

Bruce's Stone (D&G TB)

Kirkcudbright (D&G TB)

Sweetheart Abbey (D&G TB)

Industry

One industry which stretched far back into the past was mining for minerals in the Lowther Hills. The tale is told that the king of France commented on the bare hills of Scotland in comparison with the fertile fields of France. 'These hills of mine produce richer fruit than any in France,' replied the Scottish king, and for dinner that day served up a plate of gold coins. There used indeed to be some gold in the hills but panning and re-panning over the years has left none for today. But for many centuries the demand for lead was enormous, for roofing, for pipes and gutters, for weapons, for ships, for paint, glass and many other vital needs. Silver, too, could be recovered from lead. At first the mineral was extracted by surface digging or from fairly simple shafts, but in the C19th new methods of drilling and smelting led to a huge increase in production with mines driven deep into the hills. Flooding was always a problem in mines and the great beam engine, unique in its survival, was one method of pumping out the water. The village of Wanlockhead, the highest in Scotland, was first built by the Quaker Company after 1710 and rebuilt by the Duke of Queensberry in the C19th. Imported lead eventually proved cheaper and further investment was abandoned.

Water, which powered much of the machinery for the mines, also drove the grain mills, then a vital part of the economy when most of the grain needed was grown locally rather than being imported. The New Abbey corn mill with its water wheel is a rare survival of the numerous mills that once served the area.

In the C18th, some efforts were made to establish an industrial base in the region, along with planned towns and villages. William Douglas established Castle Douglas with a cotton mill, a brewery and tanneries, laying out the town with three parallel streets and five intersecting. James Murray of Broughton founded Gatehouse-of-Fleet as a centre of the textile industry, with four spinning and weaving mills employing more than 500 people. By the 1790s there were in addition two tanneries, a soap works and a brewery. Competition from other mills in more easily accessible places, however, discouraged the operators after Murray's death.

Spinning, weaving and knitting of wool, based securely on a local raw material, was much more successful and by 1810 a large-scale hosiery manufacture was centred on Dumfries. The production of knitwear is still busily alive today, some places specialising in mohair and luxury garments, much of it for export. During the last century, also, a number of Victorian mills were built in the Langholm area for the production of fine tweed, already a well established tradition on hand looms. Langholm is now the centre of the region's wool trade. The shops associated with the woollen mills here and in the regions of Moffat, Dumfries and Newton Stewart, offer a wide range of knitwear, tweed and other items, often at very reasonable prices.

The Galloway Hydro-Electric Scheme was built between 1931 and 1935, with a series of seven dams, raising the water level of some lochs and creating, as well, to improve appearance a completely new one at Clatteringshaws, with tunnels to connect parts of the system, a brilliant engineering feat with its five power stations and eleven turbo- generators still serving the public after more than 50 years.

BLADNOCH DISTILLERY TOURS Bladnoch, A714 S of Wigtown. Guided tours of this Lowland distillery, which makes a unique single malt whisky. Weekdays 10am to 4pm.

CREEBRIDGE MOHAIR MILL SHOP Creebridge, Newton Stewart. Tours of the mill with explanations of the manufacturing process. Weekdays 9am to 5pm.

GLEN CREE MILL SHOP Off King Street, Newton Stewart. Conducted tours of the mill on factory working days only 10am to 2.30pm. Shop open 9am to 5pm.

MUSEUM OF SCOTTISH LEAD MINING Wanlockhead, on B797 (a turning off A76 S of Sanquhar). Fascinating indoor museum with displays of minerals, tools and miner's home. Also open air museum with walk-in mine, water tunnel, unique beam engine, smelt mill, tramways and water lades, 1756 miners' library, cottages. All you would like to know about lead mining. Open in season, 11am to 4.30pm, but museum and walk-in mine close earlier.

NEW ABBEY CORN MILL New Abbey, A710 S of Dumfries. Working C18th corn mill with C19th additions, with water wheel, grindstones, sieves and hoppers, all complete. Open daily in season, limited opening in winter.

TONGLAND TOUR A711 just N of Kirkcudbright. Audio visual presentation of planning and building of the hydro-electric scheme followed by brief tour of the power station and visit to dam and fish ladder. Tours available in summer only and must be pre-booked.
Telephone Kirkcudbright 30114.

Crafts and Local Produce

Visitors who see the large numbers of sheep in the fields or grazing on the open moorland of the hills will not be surprised to discover that weaving and knitting of wool are part of a long tradition in this area. The river Tweed, a famous name in cloth making, although it flows in a different direction, rises not far from the source of the Annan, while in former years the knitting of hosiery was a major occupation in the Dumfries region. Today visitors are able to choose from a wide selection of woven and knitted goods. There are mill shops to be explored in Langholm, Dumfries and Newton Stewart - one of them was busy in recent years making thousands of scarves for export to Russia, which must surely be a guarantee of their warmth. The mills, of course, are producing machine made goods, but visitors will also be able to find hand knitted garments, some in the finely detailed patterns traditional in the Shetlands, some in warm Icelandic wool and in the bold colours of the Norwegian style, as well as in the complicated Aran tradition. Many people go home delighted with a tweed jacket, a kilt or a skirt, and often take smaller items, socks, gloves, hats and scarves as presents from Scotland.

It is interesting to find that there are a number of gem cutting and jewellery making workshops in the district, where you can find gifts ranging from inexpensive items, beautifully made but not using precious stones, to costly pieces of silver or gold set with gems and made to customers' special requirements. Whichever part you are in, Castle Douglas, Kirkcudbright or Stranraer, you will find examples of this local craft. One of the best centres, offering a wide range of prices, with a great deal of choice will be at Creetown. Here, of course, is the well-known Gem Rock Museum and there visitors can watch the delicate art of gem cutting, done so that each stone is shown to its best advantage, and see the final result in its setting. Creetown, too, is the home of the eminent silver-smith John Prince, who has demonstrated the art to Her Majesty th Queen, and whose work is to be found in such places as the University of Glasgow and the Vatican. He works in gold and silver, using semi-precious stones, and will execute work to your own design - so if you have some very special occasion to celebrate, he may be the man for you to visit. In the square here also is the Craft Centre, where you will find a range of gifts and souvenirs, including wooden jewellery hand-made on the premises, as well as other jewellery, pottery, toys and knitwear or tweed - something for everyone, in fact.

Pottery is to be found in a number of locations along the coast and also inland and is always popular with visitors. It is worth visiting the Gracefield Arts Centre in Dumfries where there is a pottery workshop. Ceramic animals may not be of much day to day use but are of infinite appeal to adults and children alike. They will be found in many shops in the area, and particularly in Langholm.

Some of the most interesting craft work of today is being done in glass with new and exciting shapes and colours being produced both for use and for ornament. In Dumfries and Galloway you will find the traditional engraved glass which makes such a good memento of a special occasion and can be commissioned to your requirements, and also glass blowing in modern shapes and with unusual colours and glazes. Look out for it in the local craft outlets.

Wooden spoons, small animals, bowls and other turned items are to be found, as well as hand -made clogs, embroidered pictures, and paintings by local artists, while sheepskins and leather goods are displayed in some shops. The craft centre at Drumlanrig alone, sited in the stable block, can offer ten different crafts, and a shop in even a small village will often display, along with the newspapers, maps and guide books, a selection of the crafts from that locality.

If you want to take something home, or if you are in self-catering accommodation, remember that Scotland is famous for good food, and here we have the finest raw materials. Home baking can be found in every town, with delicious pies, pasties, bridies and shortbread, all traditional Scottish fare. Special marmalades and pickles are to be found, while Scots haggis, Ayrshire bacon and Galloway beef are names which ensure excellence. A particular speciality of this region is, of course, smoked salmon. You can get it, cured and home smoked in the traditional manner by the man who caught it. At Wamphray, south of Moffat, is the tempting establishment of Alandale Game, who are licensed game dealers. They use only local products, of the finest quality, finished in the traditional Scottish manner. Here you can buy ready prepared game of all kinds, hand raised game pies or venison, and the finest smoked salmon - or fresh salmon if you prefer it. If you are cooking for yourself on your holiday, make sure you enjoy Scottish fare, or if you are on your way home, take something to remind you of the taste of Scotland. And don't forget your bottle of Lowland whisky.

The hills of the Galloway Forest Park are popular with walkers (D&G TB)

The impressive remains of Caerlaverock Castle (D&G TB)

The beautiful setting of Wanlockhead – the region's highest village (D&G TB)

History and interesting architecture amidst the colour of Threave Gardens (D&G TB)

In the past it was necessary to define the boundaries of a town and to defend it against marauders - as often as not, your neighbours. This need developed into the ancient ceremony of common riding, when a mass of riders would patrol the boundaries, usually known as marches, of the town. In places this ancient ceremony is still performed annually, though fortunately now without the threat of enemies. Langholm, Annan, Lockerbie and Sanquhar all have spectacular processions in summer, fluttering banners and pageantry recalling the stirring deeds of the past.

Lockerbie combines its common riding with a gala and many of the other towns also have gala or civic weeks. The Dumfries Guid Nychburris (Good Neighbours) Festival includes a common riding with a week of festivities, and the crowning of the Queen of the South. Galas combine processions, music, fancy dress, entertainments, competitions and sports, something for everybody to enjoy. Some, like Lochmaben, make a special point of events for children. Whatever part of the region you are in, from Gretna to Stranraer, in larger towns like Newton Stewart or smaller centres like New Galloway, there will be some traditional entertainments where you will be most welcome to join in the fun. The Summer Festivities at Kirkcudbright and Castle Douglas extend throughout the holiday season.

Agricultural Shows are another tradition of the region. Here you can learn what a champion Blackface ram or a prize-winning Belted Galloway should look like, and admire displays of massive onions or perfectly matched tomatoes. Farm machinery will be on show, and traders set up stalls selling everything from farmyard boots to ice-cream. But shows are not only for farmers. You will find baking, knitting, painting or craftwork to admire, and beautiful floral arrangements on display. There may well be sheep-dogs at work or drystane dyking competitions (stone wall building) or horse jumping to watch. Many places, from Langholm in the hills to Wigtown on the coast have their own individual show each year. Other popular events will be sheep-dog trials, or the Dumfries and Galloway Horse Show at Castle Douglas, and the three-day Horse Driving Trials at Drumlanrig.

The Galloway Games at Stranraer include traditional contests from the Highlands, which require strength and skill, like tossing the caber and putting the shot, as well as the energetic and colourful highland dancing, with the stirring sound of the bag-pipes. Very different and highly entertaining are the Scottish Alternative Games at Parton, Loch Ken, a highlight of which is the World Gird and Cleek Championship, where the competitors line up with old-fashioned iron hoops and sticks.

The sea-coast, also, enjoys its traditional pastimes and contests. Another World Championship is that of Flounder Tramping at Palnackie, where competitors have to find their catch with their toes by paddling in the silt of the estuary. This really is a traditional way of catching flat-fish! There are a number of angling festivals and contests throughout the year at Kirkcudbright and Lochryan, and Portpatrick reminds us of our debt to the sea rescue services by a special Lifeboat Week. Kippford, a yachting centre, has a regatta which is fun to watch, even if the manoeuvres of the boats are puzzling to the uninitiated.

Golf was already so popular in Scotland by 1457 that the authorities objected to it for taking up time which might be better spent on the more necessary sport of archery. King James IV, though issuing an edict in 1491 against 'golfe, or uther sik unprofitabill sportis' was himself a very keen player of the game, as his treasurer's accounts show, and one of the charges against Mary Queen of Scots was that she was seen playing golf a few days after her husband's murder, thus showing her indiffernece to the crime. The numerous golf clubs in the region have a series of special matches and trophies throughout the season, attracting competitors from far afield. At various localities, also, there are road races, camnoe races or cycle races - remember that the bicycle was invented here, and look out for special displays and events to celebrate its invention some 150 years ago.

As well as the traditional festivals which have been celebrated over the years, there are now special festivals of the arts, music and jazz. The Dumfries and Galloway Arts Festival in early summer is one of the important regional arts festivals in Scotland and provides a wide choice of plays, poetry readings, concerts and dance throughout the region. The summer holiday season brings a music festival in Stranraer and a jazz festival in Dumfries.

Visits by a regiment associated with the area, a pageant to mark a special anniversary or centenary, or the realistic re-enactment of some historic event all add to the colourful life of the region. Be sure to get a list of events from the local tourist office.

Tales and Legends

It was once firmly believed that the barnacle geese, which winter in thousands in the Solway Firth, were hatched from trees. As late as 1597 Gerard, in his famous Herball, writes 'Of the Goose Tree, Barnacle Tree or the Tree bearing geese' with a picture of a goose standing beside a branch growing very recognisable barnacles. He describes tha barnacles growing and opening and 'next come the legs of the bird hanging out, and as it groweth greater it openeth the shell by degrees, till at length it is all come forth and hangeth only by the bill; in short space after it cometh to full maturitie, and falleth into the sea, where it gathereth feathers and groweth to a fowle bigger than a Mallard'. Those that fell on land died. Pope Pius II in the C15th was disappointed to be told that such trees grew only in the Orkneys (then a remote unknown region). An advantage to churchmen and monks was that barnacle geese, not being 'born of the flesh' but of vegetable origin, could be eaten during the Lenten fast when meat was prohibited. This belief persisted well into the 1670s, though later editions of Gerard do suggest there might be 'another originall' because some Hollanders seeking a North West passage to China had come to their surprise upon an island where there were 'abundance of geese' sitting on eggs!

The Covenanters believed implicitly in every word of the Bible, in which the Book of Exodus states, 'Thou shalt not suffer a witch to live'. Visitors now park their cars at Whitesands car park. It was here that in 1669 nine women were executed as witches, condemned 'to be stranglit at the stakes till they be dead, and thereafter their bodies to be burnt to ashes'. Another way of disposing of a witch was by drowning, or by putting her into a barrel of tar, setting light to it and rolling it blazing down a hill. Witches could be accused of casting evil spells by muttering; of just walking past an animal, which then sickened and died; of doing evil to a person by making a manikin and burning it in a fire with spells and incantations; of talking to the devil 'in the shape of a black beetle'; of 'changing herself into a bat'. One tale relates how a servant girl was attacked by a huge cat, clawing and scratching. She just managed to escape by throwing a pan of boiling water over the animal. Later she found her mistress groaning in bed with scald marks exactly where the boiling water had touched the cat. Another tale is told of a young man, out with a gun, who saw a hare. It showed no alarm at his approach but though he fired several shots at it, they all missed. When he returned home, his mother said to him, 'Would you have shot your mother, my son?' Thereafter he was stricken with paralysis so that he could not rise from his bed nor speak to any stranger. The witch did this to keep her secret, for when she died he was able to get up and follow her coffin.

An often told tale is that of Sawney Bean who lived with his wife and children in a remote cave by the sea, a rude and churlish lot. About this time a lone traveller would sometimes vanish, or a workman set out for a day's work but never arrive. These strange disappearances worried the neighbourhood, especially as the numbers of missing people increased, until sometimes an entire family or a whole group of travellers would vanish, never to be seen again. Meantime Sawney Bean's family grew, until there were now grandchildren as well in the cave. One day a man and his wife going home from a fair were set upon by a wild gang of men and women. The wife was quickly killed and the man was horrified to see one of her attackers immediately start to drink her blood. He too would have been killed except for the arrival of a large party of other people also returning from the fair. The attackers, men and women, fled - to Sawney Bean's cave. Soldiers were sent for, for now the secret of the missing persons was revealed. Sawney Bean and his family were cannibals. The horrific cave was a grisly larder, where human limbs hung drying from racks or lay pickled in barrels of brine! After a desperate fight Sawney Bean and his family were taken away to be executed.

The most hated persecutor of the Covenanters was Grierson of Lag. After his death, when his coffin was placed on the hearse to be taken to the church for burial, a black crow flew down onto it, refusing to be driven off, and accompanied it on its way. The horses refused to move and stood shaking and shivering. When at last they were whipped into starting, they set off at a terrified gallop, with the coffin banging and rattling on the rough road. Before the church door they reared up to a sudden halt and fell dead in their traces. That same evening men on a boat at sea saw what they thought at first was a great ship on the horizon. But as it drew nearer, they saw to their amazement that it was not a ship but a huge black state coach drawn by six jet black horses, being driven at a furious speed over the waves. The men cowered down terrified, but one braver than the rest managed to call out the usual greeting to a passing vessel, 'Whither bound, whence from?' Loud and clear above the noise of the storm came the reply, 'Dumfries, from Hell, to tryst with Lag'.

Relaxing on the water near Threave Castle (D&G TB)

Sailing at Kippford is a popular sport (D&G TB)

Tremendous expanses of sandy beach at Sandyhills (D&G TB)

The rocky headlands and cliffs at Portpatrick (D&G TB)

Gardens of the Area

The gardens of Dumfries and Galloway are of exceptional richness and variety, so that here within a few miles visitors can find all sorts of plants, bog or rock, camellias or palms. With most of the gardens spread along the southern coastline, they enjoy the benefits of a high rainfall and the warmth brought to Scotland's west coast by the North Atlantic currents. Though winds can be strong, severe frosts are rare, and many plants from more southern climes flourish here an advantage which has inspired the Edinburgh Royal Botanic Garden to establish an out-station in the area. Whether you are interested in the plants themselves, or in garden design, or whether you just want to enjoy a walk in beautiful and tranquil surroundings, the gardens of the area contain all that you could wish for. The mildness of the climate means that spring comes early, and that autumn lingers longer than in other parts of Scotland, so that gardens may be enjoyed over many months of the year.

Styles of gardens vary from more formal layouts like those at Drumlanrig, Ardwell House or Castle Kennedy, to the more natural forms of Galloway House or the new garden at Glenwhan. In the gardens of south-west Scotland, we can find a balance between the exuberance of nature and the restraining hand of the gardener.

LOGAN BOTANIC GARDEN Port Logan, south of Stranraer, off B7065. Situated on the narrow promontary known as the Mull of Galloway, the Logan Botanic Garden enjoys the warming influence of the sea.

The Botanic Garden occupies a small area in the heart of a much larger landscape which was laid out in the C18th and C19th as a setting for Logan House. The earlier ancestral home of the McDouall family, Balzieland Castle, had burned down in 1500, and its ruins may still be sen within the Botanic Garden. Today's Logan House, which is a private residence, now lies to the north of the Botanic Garden.

The garden which we see today falls into two quite distinct halves, one a walled garden containing a number of formal features including a water garden, the other an adjacent woodland garden laid out in a more informal way. The development of the garden began in the 1860s with the construction of the walled garden.

It was in the 1870s that Agnes McDouall began the collection of plants which formed the basis of today's garden. Her two sons, Kenneth and Douglas, inherited her love of gardening, and continued to add to the collections at Logan until well into the 1930s. On the death of Kenneth McDouall in 1945 the estate was inherited by a cousin of the family, Sir Ninian Buchan Hepburn, while the house and garden were acquired by Mr Olf Hambro. Mr Hambro did much to repair the ravages of the war years. On his death the garden was administered by a trust, while the house was eventually bought by Sir Ninian Buchan Hepburn.

In 1969 the Hambro Trust gifted the walled garden and some of the adjacent areas of woodland to the Department of Agriculture and Fisheries for Scotland, to be developed as an out-station of the Royal Botanic Garden in Edinburgh. Logan's outstanding feature was its warm climate, which allowed tender plants to grow in the open air, rather than under glass as would have been necessary in the harsher conditions of the east coast.

When visiting the Logan Botanic Garden, one should remember that this is a botanic garden, designed for the scientific study of plants. Though the walled garden contains a number of beds and borders, these should not be compared with possibly more colourful gardens elsewhere. The walled garden has been developed to create a variety of habitats, including a water garden, rock garden and peat garden. The garden has many plants not often to be seen growing out of doors in our climate. Among the most striking and memorable sights are the dramatic tree ferns and cabbage palms. Plants from the Mediterranean and from various parts of the southern hemisphere are well represented, as are those from the Himalayas. In the woodland garden the 'Gunnera Bog' forms a striking feature, dominated by a mass of giant rhubarb-like leaves. The botanical treasures of this garden are too many to name, but both the expert and the amateur will find a vist a fascinating and rewarding experience. When visiting the garden, you can buy an excellent illustrated handbook which will guide you around the most interesting features, and will pick out plants of special interest to be found at different times of year.

The Logan Botanic Garden is open daily between April and September. Refreshments are available, and facilities are provided for disabled visitors. The neighbouring gardens around the new Logan House may be open occasionally under Scotland's Gardens Scheme, but are not normally accessible at other times.

ARBIGLAND GARDENS South of Dumfries on A710 coast road. From the older area of formally planted woodland which surrounds the house, a broad-walk leads down to the shore and a sandy bay. Near the shore, the grandmother of the present owner created a sunken garden and laid out terraces leading to the 'House on the Shore'. A guided walk leads visitors to different parts of the garden, where plants include rhododendrons, camellias and hostas. It was here in a cottage on the estate that John Paul Jones - naval adventurer and later admiral of the American Navy - was born, and worked with his father who was the estate gardener. Picnic and play areas, and a rustic tea-room make this an ideal place to bring the family. The gardens are open on Tuesday, Thursday and Sunday afternoons from May to September.

ARDWELL GARDENS South of Stranraer on A716. A visit to this garden can easily be combined with one to the nearby Logan Botanic Garden. A formal layout around the house gradually merges into informal shrubberies and woodlands where spring flowers abound. Azaleas, camellias and rhododendrrons flower a little later on. A new water garden has been developed, and walks take the visitor around the main lake, or to viewpoints overlooking Luce Bay to the east. The garden is open daily from March to October.

BROUGHTON HOUSE High Street, Kirkcudbright. This is a small town garden adjacent to Broughton House, which was formerly the home of the artist E.A.Hornel (1864-1933). A great lover of flowers, Hornel landscaped part of the gardens to resemble a Japanese sanctuary, inspired by his earlier visits to the Far East. There are also more conventional borders. The gallery and garden are open from Easter to mid-October.

CASTLE KENNEDY GARDENS East of Stranraer on A75. The gardens occupy a neck of land between two lochs. They were first laid out in formal style in the 1730s by the 2nd Earl of Stair, perhaps influenced by the famous gardens of Versailles, for he had earlier been British Ambassador to France. Though neglected at the end of the C18th, the gardens were restored in the C19th and have since been added to and developed, while retaining the formal structure. The ruins of Castle Kennedy stand in the gardens, while the home of the present Earl of Stair, the elaborate C19th Lochinch Castle, lies to the north. The gardens are famed for their rhododendrons, azaleas, magnolias and for their splendid trees and avenues. Refreshments are available. The gardens are open from April to September.

DRUMLANRIG CASTLE Near Thornhill, north of Dumfries. Best known for its magnificent pink sandstone castle and dramatic highland setting, Drumlanrig also boasts fine gardens. The gardens close to the castle are formal in character, and include a parterre restored to its 1747 plan. Elsewhere a large rock garden has recently been replanted, and much work done on creating borders, lawns, terraces and woodland glades. The woodlands contain early introductions to Britain from other countries, including the Douglas Fir and the 'Gingko' or Maidenhair tree. The gardens are open throughout most of the summer.

GALLOWAY HOUSE GARDENS At Garlieston, south of Wigtown, off A714. The gardens at Galloway House stretch down to a sandy bay. An attractive mixture of deciduous and coniferous trees fringes the shore and surrounds the house, sheltering a variety of ornamental and flowering shrubs. Disabled visitors can be accommodated. Open daily throughout the year.

GLENWHAN At Dunragit, east of Stranraer on A75. This is a new and unusual garden created since 1979 on a hill-top overlooking Luce Bay. Herbaceous, bog and rock gardens have been developed around two lochans (small lakes), a major achievement in a comparatively short time. Teas are available. Open daily April to September.

KIRROUGHTREE FOREST GARDEN East of Newton Stewart on A712. This area of woodland has been developed by the Forestry Commission as an arboretum, with more than 60 different types of tree gathered from around the world. There are way-marked walks. Open all year.

MAXWELTON HOUSE Near Moniaive, north-west of Dumfries on B729. One of few inland gardens in the area. There are colourful displays of bulbs in spring, followed by many flowering trees and shrubs. There are also fine hothouses. The house is open in July and August and there is a chapel and small museum. Gardens open Monday to Thursday, April to September.

THREAVE GARDEN Near Castle Douglas. One of Scotland's outstanding gardens, see ' National Trust for Scotland Properties'.

There are many other beautiful gardens in the area which are open occasionally under **SCOTLAND'S GARDENS SCHEME**. Look out in the local tourist office or the local paper, and keep your eyes open for the distinctive yellow posters and signs which indicate a special open day for an otherwise private garden.

The Burns Centre and its riverside setting (D&G TB)   Sanquhar's famous Post Office (D&G TB)

The magnificence of hills, forest and lakes near Clatteringshaws (D&G TB)

The Cairnholy Prehistoric Monument has a magnificent setting (D&G TB)

Watersports on Loch Ken are a popular pastime (D&G TB)

Dumfries and Galloway occupies a strip of land some 145km (90 miles) from east to west and no more than 70km (45 miles) from north to south. Within this small compass there is a great variety of habitats, whether along its deeply indented coastline, in the rich agricultural lowlands or among the hills and forests.

There are the sheltered bays and estuaries of the Solway coast, which enjoy the warming influence of the sea; lowland areas with a rich mixture of grassland, arable and woodland; blanket bog and heather moor; lochs and rivers; even sub-arctic conditions in the highest hills, stretching from the Rhinns of Kells in the west, through the Lowther Hills to Eskdalemuir in the east. To the south, on the Mull of Galloway, plants from the Mediterranean thrive in the Logan Botanic Garden, while little more than 48km (30 miles) to the north, the red deer, grouse and mountain hares flourish among the hills.

Winter brings immense numbers of birds to feed and roost on the mud-flats and salt-marshes of the Solway coast, while spring and early summer bring life to the cliffs, woodlands and upland areas. Largely unspoiled by coastal development or industrialisation, the rivers and estuaries of Dumfries and Galloway are relatively unpolluted. Only acidification of the soil and water, perhaps, causes concern, for this natural process is being accelerated by the planting of conifers on the northern hills.

The rich variety of wildlife and habitats in the area is reflected in the number of reserves, managed by a range of public and voluntary bodies. These include the Forestry Commission (FC), Nature Conservancy Council (NCC), National Trust for Scotland (NTS), Royal Society for the Protection of Birds (RSPB), Scottish Wildlife Trust (SWT) and Wildfowl Trust (WT), together with local authorities and others. Access to some of the most fragile habitats is naturally restricted - blanket bog, for instance, does not benefit from the tramp of human feet! At other reserves access is by permit only, but there are many places where access is open and unrestricted except during the breeding season.

The following paragraphs do no more than introduce you to the main types of habitat, and pick out some of the most accessible sites. Remember, however, that wildlife does not confine itself to reserves! Those with a keen eye and a little patience, prepared to explore a little away from the crowds, will find themselves richly rewarded.

ALONG THE COAST

Don't allow yourself to think that history is the only thing to see along the Solway Coast Heritage Trail. Indeed, just as some of the historic sites put up their shutters for the winter, some of the area's wildlife sites are gearing up for their busiest time. (Sites E-W).

CAERLAVEROCK WILDFOWL REFUGE (WT & NCC). On B725 from Annan to Dumfries. One of the most important areas in Britain for wintering wildfowl and wading birds. Among the highlights are the 8,000 or so barnacle geese which fly here from their Arctic breeding grounds each year to join many other species of birds which make use of the rich pickings to be had on the huge salt-marshes and mud-flats. Guided visits are organised between mid-September and April.

DRUMMAINS REED BED RESERVE (SWT) is across the Nith estuary from Caerlaverock, on A710, south of Dumfries. Here a hide overlooks the reed beds. Visitors in winter will see wildfowl and waders, while summer brings nesting lapwing, redshank, terns and other marshland birds.

SOUTHWICK COAST RESERVE (SWT) On A710 south of Dumfries. Here an area of ancient oak-wood survives on an old cliff, now raised above sea-level. At its foot, the Needle's Eye and Lot's Wife form interesting geological features.

ROCKCLIFFE (NTS) is a short distance further along the same road. Here there is a bird sanctuary on Rough Island. This stretch of coastline can be enjoyed from the coast path between Rockcliffe and nearby Kippford.

SKYREBURN AQUARIUM is west of Gatehouse-of- Fleet, on A75. Here you can be introduced to the variety of freshwater and marine life which is all about, but seldom seen, in the sea, rivers and lochs.

THE MULL OF GALLOWAY (RSPB) The best time for a visit is probably in late spring and early summer. A reserve has been created here to protect the sea-birds which nest on the rugged cliffs - among them fulmars, cormorants, kittiwakes, razor-bills & guillemots.

LOGAN FISH POND At Port Logan, B7065. This is a tidal pool cut into the rock in 1800 as a fresh fish larder for Logan House. The fish become so tame that you can stroke them. The pond is open on Mondays, Wednesdays, Fridays and Sundays in summer.

THE LOWLANDS

In the lowland areas of Dumfries and Galloway few areas have escaped exploitation, as farmers have sought to make the best use of the relatively rich lowland soils for grazing or cultivation. Only where the land is too wet or too steep to allow easy access have more natural habitats survived.

WETLAND SITES are of special importance. Among those that have escaped drainage are:
CASTLE AND HIGHTAE LOCHS RESERVE (Annandale and Eskdale DC) near Lochmaben, where mixed woodland surrounds two nutrient-rich lochs.
THREAVE WILDFOWL REFUGE (NTS) by the River Dee, just west of Castle Douglas, which is open from November to March and provides carefully screened viewing points from which to enjoy the wintering waterfowl which use the reserve. Indeed, the beautiful Dee valley, bordering Loch Ken, is rich in wildlife and it includes
THE KEN-DEE MARSHES RESERVE (RSPB) Though access is restricted, views may be had of this area from many points on the A713 and A762 roads on either side of the valley.
FOUNTAINBLEAU AND LADYPARK RESERVE (SWT) On the north-eastern outskirts of Dumfries, a reserve has been established on the site of a former loch, now overgrown with vegetation, and supporting a rich area of birch, willow and alder woodland. A trail has been laid out to draw attention to interesting features.

LOWLAND WOODLAND which has survived past exploitation is rare and reserves have been established to protect remaining fragments at:
STENHOUSE WOOD RESERVE (SWT) near Tynron, off A702 between Thornhill and Moniaive.
CASTRAMON RESERVE (SWT) by B796, north of Gatehouse-of-Fleet.
THE FORESTRY COMMISSION cares for some sites where areas of valuable wildlife habitat have been incorporated into new afforestation, and are managed in such a way as to protect and enhance their value. Such are:
MABIE FOREST (FC) S of Dumfries on A71.
PLANTAIN LOCH (FC) South of Dalbeattie.
PENNINGHAME (FC) North-west of Newton Stewart, on B7027.

Though many of the wildlife sites mentioned above are accessible, please remember that some habitats are easily damaged. For your own safety, and to protect the wildlife, keep to the paths provided. Heed the notices and take special care during the breeding season.

THE UPLANDS

The northern hills stand in dramatic contrast to the richer land to the south. Above and between the forested areas, boggy wastes lead up to rugged hills such as the Merrick, where in the northern and eastern corries grow arctic-alpine plants. This is country for the dedicated walker only - properly equipped and prepared for dramatic changes in the weather. This is the land of the curlew, the golden plover and the snipe, hunted over by harriers, peregrines and even golden eagles.

New afforestation brings successive changes to the uplands. New habitats are created while the trees are young, but the tree canopy soon closes and shuts out the wildlife, except along the forest margins. More attention is now paid to conservation than in the past, with foresters leaving some areas unplanted. Felling again alters the scene.

THE GREY MARE'S TAIL (NTS) North of Moffat off A708. An upland site noted for its flora and for its herd of wild goats, probably the descendants of domestic animals allowed to go wild at some time in the past. Visitors should be careful to keep to the paths in this area.
GLENTROOL (FC) has fine areas of mixed oak and birch wood, survivals of original woodland cover at Lochead, with pleasant trails.
THE WOOD OF CREE RESERVE (RSPB) North of Newton Stewart on A714 also has original woodland cover and a variety of woodland birds.
THE WILD GOAT PARK (FC) By the Queen's Way, A712 from Newton Stewart to New Galloway. The goats are easily seen on the steep hillside.
THE RED DEER RANGE (FC) is just beyond the the Wild Goat Park. The Forestry Commission provides facilities to watch these elusive creatures grazing on lichens and mosses in a semi-natural habitat of 250 hectares.
THE GALLOWAY DEER MUSEUM (FC) also on A712. As well as information about deer, this museum has displays about the general forest management, ecology and wildlife, including a live trout exhibit. Open Apr to Sept.

Summer or winter, there is plenty to see. Some sites have hides or way-marked walks. Some even have staff who can give you up-to-the-minute information on what there is to be seen. When packing for your holiday, remember your binoculars, waterproofs, and a plentiful supply of insect repellent for warm evenings.

The peace, beauty and tranquility of Carlingwark Loch (D&G TB)

The amazing colour and beauty of Threave Gardens (D&G TB)

The National Trust for Scotland was founded in 1931 with a view to the preservation of 'land and buildings in Scotland of natural beauty or historic interest'. It now owns or manages more than 100 sites and properties throughout the country. Members of the National Trust (England and Wales) are admitted free. Full details of Trust properties can be obtained from: National Trust for Scotland, 5 Charlotte Square, Edinburgh, EH2 4DU.

THREAVE GARDEN Just west of Castle Douglas, signposted from A75. Outstanding among the Trust's properties in Dumfries and Galloway. Compared to other garden properties in the Trust's care Threave is of recent origin, having been designed as a teaching garden. Although the house and garden were acquired in 1948, it was not until 1960 that the School of Gardening was opened. It now trains up to eight students every year, many of whom go on to work in other Trust gardens. A range of different garden types has been created, to give students a variety of experience. There are woodland, peat, heath and rock gardens, a rose garden and orchard, as well as herbaceous borders. There are also a collection of grasses and an arboretum. Threave is probably best known for its magnificent collection of some 200 different types of daffodil. There is a visitor centre, exhibition and shop, together with facilities for disabled visitors. The gardens are open throughout the year, though the visitor facilities are only open from March to October.

THREAVE COUNTRYSIDE WALK This reminds visitors that the garden is but one part of a much larger estate administered by the Trust. The half-hour circuit takes in the surrounding farmland and countryside.

THREAVE CASTLE This lies some distance to the north on an island in the River Dee. This massive stronghold of the Douglas family was built by Archibald the Grim. The ruined castle, reached by a walk and a ferry crossing, is now in the care of the Historic Buildings and Monuments, Scottish Development Department. See 'Castles and Tower Houses'.

CARLYLE'S BIRTHPLACE In Ecclefechan, off A74, south of Lockerbie. Birthplace of the noted historian, essayist and social reformer Thomas Carlyle (1795-1881), this is a robust artisan's cottage with an arched entrance, built by Carlyle's father and uncle, both of them master masons, in about 1791. Carlyle manuscripts and other memorabilia are on display. The house is open from late March to the end of October.   **ROCKCLIFFE** South of Dalbeattie, off A710. This unites several Trust properties. These include the **MOTE** (or motte) **OF MARK**, an ancient hill fort overlooking the River Urr (see 'Prehistoric and Early Sites), and nearby **ROUGH ISLAND**, now managed by the Trust as a bird sanctuary. Between Rockcliffe and neighbouring Kippford is **MUCKLE LANDS and JUBILEE PATH**, a rough and picturesque stretch of coastline. These sites are all within the East Stewartry National Scenic Area, one of three such areas in Dumfries and Galloway.

VENNIEHILL Main Street in Gatehouse-of-Fleet. This small field encompasses a hill-top viewpoint with fine views over the rich and varied countryside around the Water of Fleet. It is included in the Fleet Valley National Scenic Area.

GLENLUCE ABBEY GLEBE North of Glenluce, signposted from A75. The Glebe is managed by the Historic Buildings and Monuments, Scottish Development Department who care for the ruins of this Cistercian abbey, founded in 1192. The remains include a fine vaulted chapter house. See 'Christian Sites and Abbeys'.

BRUCE'S STONE By A712 Queen's Way from Newton Stewart to New Galloway. Not to be confused with the monument of the same name in Glentrool. This large granite boulder marks the site of another successful encounter between Robert Bruce and his English foes.

GREY MARE'S TAIL North of Moffat, by A708. The Tail Burn forms an impressive 200ft waterfall as it descends from Loch Skeen to join the Moffat Water below. The area is known for its wild flowers, and for a rare herd of wild goats. The paths to the falls and Loch Skeen are dangerous, and should only be attempted by those who are properly equipped.

GUIDED WALKS

At **Threave Garden**, the National Trust for Scotland have a number of guided walks and garden demonstrations at intervals from April to October.

At **The Grey Mare's Tail** there are regular guided walks, led by the Trust's Ranger/Naturalist staff, during July and August. Participants must be properly equipped for hill-walking.

Full details of walks may be found in the Trust's 'Events' calendar, or in the programme of Ranger/Naturalist Guided Walks.

It was marriage and romance that made Gretna famous. English marriage laws were strict but in Scotland anyone over the age of sixteen could be married without parental consent. All that was required was a simple declaration before a responsible witness - a blacksmith, for instance. Several houses in Gretna Green, the first place over the border, were ready to oblige, and many elopements, including that of the famous huntsman John Peel, ended happily here, while the village has provided novelists with innumerable romantic stories of lovers driving furiously to Gretna Green pursued by irascible fathers or guardians. (For more details, see 'Three Unusual Museums').

Bypassed now by the busy A74 and A75 trunk roads, Gretna makes a good centre for exploration, with good hotels and a large and pleasant caravan site nearby. Riding is also available in the locality. The Blacksmith's Shop and other marriage houses are at the old village of Gretna Green where every facility is offered to visitors, confirming all their ideas of romantic Scotland, complete with kilted bagpipe player, opportunities to reaffirm their own vows, and a display of carriages and coaches, which brought so many eloping couples to the village. The modern village of Gretna, a short distance away, is an interesting example of C20th town planning, for it was built to house munition workers during the First World War. Spaciously laid out, with a large green, the houses, in a simple neo-georgian style, are symmetrically arranged, and experience from here was later incorporated in the Housing and Town Planning Act of 1919, the source of many of the new towns built in subsequent years.

Surrounded by level and fertile farming country, Gretna is within easy reach of the Solway coast, famous world wide for the wealth of the bird life in winter, a place where the tides race in over miles of sand and mud flats, and where the interesting 'haaf' net fishing can sometimes be seen. Within reach, too, are the hills and dales of northern Dumfries and Galloway, while Carlisle, Hadrian's Wall and the English Lake District are only a short drive away.

Within a few miles the visitor can see the Ruthwell Cross, an internationally admired relic from the Dark Ages, or the medieval Merkland Cross, or visit the great castles of Caerlaverock and Lochmaben, or Carlyle's Birthplace at Ecclefechan. The road to Longtown passes Solway Moss, the scene of a disastrous defeat of the Scots in 1542, which led to the death of the king, leaving his only heir the infant Mary Queeen of Scots. Northwards from Longtown, or alternatively reached by a minor road from Kirkpatrick Fleming, is Canonbie, and beyond that Langholm and the beautiful and remote Eskdale.

Known in former days as 'the debatable lands', these dales were the homes and lairs of the notorious border reivers. Taking advantage of the remote country, impossible for the soldiers of either the Scottish or the English king to patrol effectively, they lived by cattle thieving and looting, and by protection rackets which have given the word 'blackmail' to our language. The ruined Hollows Tower and Gilnockie Tower are reminders of their forbidding power and were former homes of the Armstrongs, among the most feared of all. Today Eskdale is the most beautiful and peaceful valley, where the road follows the course of the Esk river, famous for its salmon and sea-trout fishing.

In the middle of the valley is Langholm, a centre of the wool trade, for these green hills are 'sheep country'. Langholm recalls its more turbulent past each year with a colourful Commons Riding, where over two hundred horsemen 'ride the Marches', to protect its boundaries. Today it is a market town, notable for its sheep and cattle sales and is also the producer of fine worsted cloth and knitwear. Visitors will enjoy a visit to a mill shop, and also to a gallery of ceramic figures and animals. Not far distant is Craigcleugh, the museum of the Scottish Explorers, where there are treasures brought back from all over the world.

The valley beyond Langholm is said by many to have the most beautiful scenery in the south of Scotland and the quiet B709 road still following the course of the river, winds through the hills which are in places heavily clothed in forest. So remote and undisturbed is it that the Tibetans exiled from their own country chose it as the place to build their monastery, the only Tibetan monastery in Britain, where, in addition to their devotions, they produce a range of artwork and crafts. Further up the valley are meteorological and seismological stations and the name of Eskdalemuir is familiar to people who listen to broadcast weather reports.

Thomas Telford, the great engineer, was born in Westerkirk, the son of a shepherd, and first went to work in Langholm. Although his life was spent travelling throughout Britain, he left money in his will for the libraries at Langholm and Westerkirk.

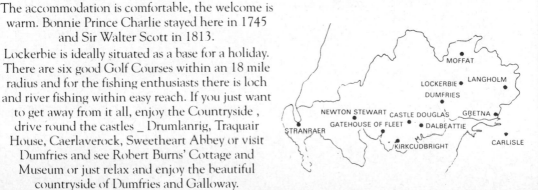

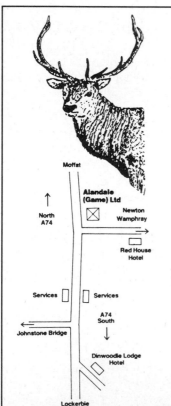

Annan, Moffat & Annandale

The river Annan starts in the Lowther Hills and flows through a wide and fertile landscape to reach the Solway Firth. This has long been a major route between England and Scotland, and today the A74 road and the Carlisle to Glasgow railway both enter Scotland at Gretna. From there they lead north-west toward the Annan and then follow the river valley past Ecclefechan, Lockerbie and Beattock. The town of Annan itself lies by the A75 route to Dumfries and Stranraer, close to the Solway Firth. Built mainly of warm red sandstone, it is a prosperous market town for the surrounding farming district of fertile low-lying fields, with their herds of black-and-white Friesian cattle. The centre of the town is a long, wide and spacious street, with narrower streets either end. The river here is still tidal and is noted for the quality of its fishing.

As well as providing comfortable hotels, the district is well provided with caravan and camping sites, either inland or on the popular Solway coast. The wide sands of the Solway attract many who enjoy a seaside holiday, with picnics, sand and paddling, although this region is not good for swimming, as the Solway here is a place of fast tides and ever-changing channels. There is plenty of other seaside entertainment, with an 18-hole golf course, and also facilities for launching boats near Annan. Summer is not the only time to visit the region, for it is the famous winter haunt of thousands of birds, including huge numbers of barnacle geese, and many nature lovers will come when special bird watching tours are organised between September and April.

This, too, is an area of great historical interest. The medieval fortress of Caerlaverock is not far distant along the coast, and that of Lochmaben is to the north, while the C15th Comlongon tower house emphasises the continual strife of former years, still remembered in the annual Riding of the Marches in Annan. One of the greatest treasures of the Dark Ages, a remarkable sculptured stone cross, is to be found in the church at Ruthwell, a place which also has associations with Robert Burns.

There is no need to follow the fast moving traffic of the A74, for the B723 road will take you to Lockerbie. It is a short detour to visit Carlyle's Birthplace at Ecclefechan, and you can also enjoy the forest and farm walks of the Hoddom Estate. Lockerbie is a good centre, within reach of the coast and also of the hills. You can follow the road up alongside the Dryfe Water and into Eskdale, or take an afternoon's exercise on the 18-hole golf course. Golf addicts will be pleased to discover that there are five other courses within fifteen miles. If you are a winter visitor, you can enjoy curling, another game of Scottish origin, on the local ice-rink.

The B7020 road follows up Annandale as the river meanders through the prosperous farmland. Close to where the Water of Ae and the Dryfe Water join the Annan is Lochmaben, the site of a great castle, now much reduced, which was of vital strategic importance in the wars between the Scots and English. Lochmaben, too, offers golf, tennis and bowls, as well as bird-watching and walks in this attractive district.

As the hills close in, the road reaches Beattock, a place most welcome to weary walkers on the Southern Upland Way. Not far from Beattock is Moffat. Situated in this dramatic landscape Moffat was once a well-known spa town, one of only two in Scotland, and it still retains the aura of a leisured past. More than once it has won an award in the Britain in Bloom Competition and visitors will enjoy the well-kept parks, the wide main street lined with interesting shops, the museum and the abundance of trees and flowers. The former baths and pump room now house the town hall.

In this peaceful ambience there are opportunities for riding, golf and tennis; there is a boating pond; there are plenty of walks, from the Southern Upland Way for dedicated walkers to guided hill walks or just pleasant strolls for the less ambitious; explore into the hills and you will find the Grey Mare's Tail Waterfall or the Devil's Beef Tub, a huge natural depression where border thieves were said to hide their stolen cattle. Go on further and you reach Beattock summit at 312m (1025ft) and the watershed, where you are near the source not only of the Annan but also of the Tweed which flows into the sea on the opposite side of Scotland.

This is the country of the sheep and the statue of the ram above the fountain in Moffat reminds the visitor of the importance of the wool trade to the economy of the area. A high point of Moffat District Gala week is the Installation of the Moffat Shepherd and Lass and the Shepherd's Ball afterwards. The Border Collie and Shepherd Centre, with sheep-dog demonstrations, is on the A701 road to Broughton. Mill shops with wool, tartan, tweed and knitwear tempt the visitor, while a number of craft outlets are to be found in the area, as well as mouth-watering displays of local and traditional Scottish foods.

Dumfries and Nithsdale

Although little is left of the medieval town, Dumfries has for long been the main centre of this region, having been given the status of a royal burgh as long ago as 1186. Prior to this date the people had been dependent on their feudal overlords, to whom they had to render labour and military service. But with the grant of a royal charter dues had to be paid only to the crown, and merchants and craftsmen achieved a considerable degree of local self-government, together with important trading rights which enabled the town to grow and prosper.

Today Dumfries is a lively place, very busy and with a good shopping centre. It is attractive, with some of the houses painted in soft colours of blue, cream, green or buff, and most of the important buildings in red sandstone, making a pleasing mixture. In the centre of the town is the Midsteeple, completed in 1708 to provide a meeting place for the town council as well as a courtroom and prison. A plaque on the outer wall gives the distances to other towns and cities to which the people of Dumfries might have wanted to travel in the C18th.

The medieval town was on one side of the Nith river, which now flows through the modern town between wide banks, and the old red sandstone bridge, dating back to the C15th, once provided an entrance with a toll house at the far end. This is known as Devorguilla's Bridge, for it was here that the Lady Devorguilla de Balliol had the first bridge built, probably of timber, in the C13th. It has to be remembered that in former years ships were able to navigate the Nith, and it was the Dumfries merchants who built the lighthouse at Southerness. In the C18th and C19th the quays downriver at Kingholm amd Glencaple were still busy with ships trading to North America, the West Indies and the Baltic.

The later Medieval period, with constant wars on the border between Scotland and England, saw Dumfries raided and burned on several occasions and little now remains from that period, the site of its once great castle being now a wooded park with only the name Castledykes to remind us of its former existence. On the northern outskirts, however, is Lincluden College, the ruined remains of a once richly established monastic foundation, still the peaceful and tranquil spot loved by Burns who addressed an imaginative poem to the ruins,
'Ye holy walls, that still sublime,
Resist the crumbling touch of time.."
Other reminders of these days are to the south-east at Caerlaverock Castle and to the south-west at Sweetheart Abbey, founded by the same Lady Devorguilla in memory of her husband. Dumfries was also the scene of a famous episode in the life of Robert Bruce, for it was at Greyfriars Monastery in Dumfries (the church has long since disappeared) that Bruce and one of his followers stabbed to death the Red Comyn, a rival claimant to the throne, thus clearing the way for Bruce's accession and his eventual defeat of the English.

The C17th saw Dumfries ruled by the Covenanters, when dancing, music and gaming were banned, attendance at church was compulsory and even 'walking idly from house to house and gossiping on the sabbath day' was considered a crime. This was the time, too, throughout northern Europe, of the great fear of witches, which saw many trials and condemnations, including, in Dumfries, the execution of nine women in one day.

A statue of Robert Burns overlooks the town's High Street, for it was in Dumfries that the poet spent the last five years of his life, and there are many interesting associations with him, the house where he lived, the tavern where he spent much of his time, and his tomb, as well as a splendid Robert Burns Centre in an old sandstone mill building by the river. The visitor can follow a Burns Heritage Trail round the sites once familiar to him.

This has always been an agricultural region with much of its economy dependent on sheep and cattle farming and Dumfries has a long tradition of an allied industry in the manufacture of knitwear and, in particular, of hosiery. While these trades still contribute much today, there have in recent years been efforts to attract a wider range of work and today a large number of light industries are at work in the area.

The town is well provided with museums and libraries which help to illuminate its history, and there is also a fascinating camera obscura which projects a moving panoramic view of the district, and an art gallery showing the work of local and contemporary artists. Dumfries is a good centre, offering the visitor all the facilities expected of an important town, including a swimming pool, parks, two golf courses, evening entertainments, nightclubs and discos, as well as good shopping and branches of major stores. The town is at the centre of an Arts Festival, with many special events, and the annual Guid Nychburris Festival, with the Crowning of the Queen of the South, is a colourful and enjoyable celebration of its warm and friendly spirit.

To the south of Dumfries is the Nith estuary, now classified as a National Scenic Area. This is a wide tidal landscape with extensive sands, mudflats and saltings which are enhanced by the contrasting coastline. Close to Dumfries is Mabie Forest, with walks and a picnic area, the wooded ridge of high ground extending above a large expanse of flats where there is a mixture of pasture and peat moss to the west of the main river channel. Further south the rich pastoral landscape around New Abbey contrasts with the hill of Criffel, its steep slopes a mixture of moorland and woodland. At New Abbey are to be found the ruins of Sweetheart Abbey, the New Abbey Corn Mill, a working mill driven by a water wheel, and the Shambellie House Museum of Costume.

The eastern shore of the estuary is less hilly and the river is bordered by open fields and marshes beside wide mud flats. The tide retreats far across these mud flats and sands and its ebbing and flowing gives the scene a constantly changing atmosphere. This wide and watery landscape is the setting for Caerlaverock Castle, its triangular shape unique in Britain, and also for the Caerlaverock Wildfowl Refuge, one of the most important areas in Britain for wildfowl and wading birds in winter.

North of Dumfries the A76 road follows the fertile valley of the Nith, past broad, well-cared for fields, indicative of a prosperous farming area. This region, too, is associated with Robert Burns for it was here that he owned a farm. As you travel north, the landscape becomes more hilly, with a mixture of deciduous and coniferous trees among the fields, and soon the long line of the Lowther Hills can be seen to the east. The main centre for this part of Nithsdale is Thornhill, a most attractive place with an unusually wide main street lined with carefully trimmed trees. The houses are a pleasant mixture of two or three storeys, giving a varied roofline, some in sandstone, some painted and with contrasting window frames, an example of the typical local architecture at its best. Visitors can enjoy golf, tennis, bowling and squash, or the less energetic pursuit of fishing either in rivers or lochs in the district.

The winged horse on top of the column in the village is the emblem of the Queensberry family whose great mansion of Drumlanrig lies to the west. It is worth making the detour to see this cross between a castle and a palace, built in pink sandstone, with numerous turrets and a sweeping entrance stair, worthy of a fairy-tale. If you are there when it is open to the public, you will find the rooms full of fine decoration and many treasures. Another house in the area is Maxwelton.

This is a country of hills and attractive glens, down which sparkling streams hurry, where the visitor can find a peaceful 'away from it all' atmosphere. At its centre, where three streams meet, is Moniaive, its painted cottages lining the street, with an old pub and market cross. From here roads lead through the hills to the next valley and to St. John's Town of Dalry, the old route from Edinburgh to Whithorn, used by pilgrims, and in later days by smugglers. Further north the hills increase in height toward Cairnsmore of Carsphairn at over 915m (2000ft).

These glens and hills provided a refuge for persecuted Covenanters, and many conventicles were held in their remote and secret places, while in Saanquhar, to the north, declarations against the king's rule were posted openly in the market place. Nithsdale District Council has produced a Covenanting Trail booklet, with a map and historical information, which takes the visitor round many of the sites associated with the Covenanters, making as well an interesting tour of Nithsdale.

Sanquhar has a golf course, a museum and many opportunities for walks and picnics among the hills, where the Southern Upland Way passes. Here, too, you can post your letters and cards in the oldest post office in the world, dating from 1763. Sanquhar's castle, of which now only traces remain, saw much conflict, and the town recalls history with an annual Riding of the Marches, the climax of its gala week.

From Sanquhar you can drive into the Lowther Hills, where several summits rise over 600m (2000ft), to the Scottish Lead Mining Museum at Wanlockhead. This is Scotland's highest village, about 450m (1500ft) above sea level, and was the source of much mineral wealth dug from the surrounding hills. Here you can find out what it meant to live in a miner's home or work in a lead mine, see a beam engine, smelt mill, waggon ways and water lades. Even without the lead mining museum the impressive Lowther hills deserve a visit. Cropped over generations by sheep, many slopes present a bare and rounded appearance. Elsewhere carefully managed heather is to be seen or forestry plantations have been introduced. Your route may run alongside a stream tumbling over stones, cross a stretch of moorland, or wind its way through the spectacular Dalveen Pass.

WHAT'S NITHSDALE GOT?
IT'S GOT THE LOT

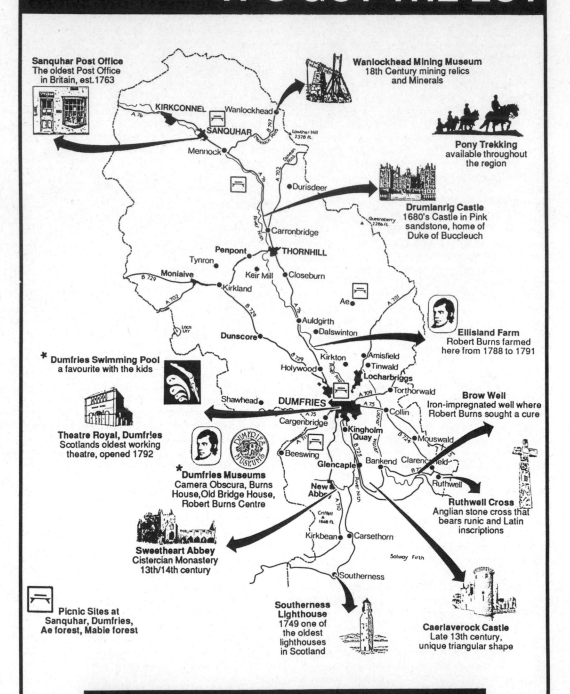

Sanquhar Post Office
The oldest Post Office in Britain, est. 1763

Wanlockhead Mining Museum
18th Century mining relics and Minerals

Pony Trekking
available throughout the region

Drumlanrig Castle
1680's Castle in Pink sandstone, home of Duke of Buccleuch

Ellisland Farm
Robert Burns farmed here from 1788 to 1791

* **Dumfries Swimming Pool**
a favourite with the kids

Theatre Royal, Dumfries
Scotlands oldest working theatre, opened 1792

* **Dumfries Museums**
Camera Obscura, Burns House, Old Bridge House, Robert Burns Centre

Brow Well
Iron-impregnated well where Robert Burns sought a cure

Ruthwell Cross
Anglian stone cross that bears runic and Latin inscriptions

Sweetheart Abbey
Cistercian Monastery 13th/14th century

Picnic Sites at Sanquhar, Dumfries, Ae forest, Mabie forest

Southerness Lighthouse
1749 one of the oldest lighthouses in Scotland

Caerlaverock Castle
Late 13th century, unique triangular shape

Map labels: KIRKCONNEL, Wanlockhead, SANQUHAR, Mennock, Lowther Hill 2378 ft., Durisdeer, Queensberry 2286 ft., Carronbridge, Penpont, THORNHILL, Tynron, Keir Mill, Closeburn, Moniaive, Kirkland, Ae, Loch Urr, Auldgirth, Dalswinton, Dunscore, Kirkton, Amisfield, Tinwald, Holywood, Locharbriggs, Shawhead, DUMFRIES, Torthorwald, Collin, Cargenbridge, Kingholm Quay, Mouswald, Beeswing, Bankend, Clarencefield, Glencaple, New Abbey, Ruthwell, Criffell 1866 ft., Kirkbean, Carsethorn, Solway Firth, Southerness

* **FOR FURTHER INFORMATION CONTACT**
NITHSDALE DISTRICT COUNCIL
DEPARTMENT OF LEISURE, RECREATION AND TOURISM
Municipal Buildings, Buccleuch Street, Dumfries Tel: 53166

Robert Burns in Dumfries

When Robert Burns moved to Dumfriesshire from Ayrshire in 1788, at the age of 29, it was in the hope that he could put behind him the financial and health problems which had been a feature of his early years. He had accepted the lease of Ellisland, a farm on the west bank of the river Nith to the north of Dumfries. After seeing to the construction of the farmhouse, Burns brought his new bride Jean Armour to live there. The 100 acres of Ellisland had been exhausted by years of grazing and overcropping, and despite Burns's best efforts to improve the land, the task proved all but impossible.

Burns had earlier taken a course of instruction as an excise officer. In 1789, leaving his wife in charge of the farm, he began work as an excise man. Constant travelling on horseback as much as 200 miles each week - in all weathers can have done little to help the health of a man already weakened by years of unremitting toil.

In 1791 Burns finally abandoned the struggle and moved to Dumfries where he became a full-time excise officer. At first he lived in a tenement in Wee Vennel, now Bank Street but then known as Stinking Vennel, but soon moved with his family into a larger house in Mill Vennel, now Burns Street.

Burns was conscientious in his work and, despite his reputation as a frequenter of taverns, he soon gained promotion. He continued to write, some of his finest songs dating from this period. His health was still poor, however, and the accumulated strains of his early life, added to domestic complications, saw him fall prey to illness in the winter of 1795-96. Despite a remedy of sea-bathing and mineral waters prescribed by his doctor, his condition grew worse and he died at his home on 21st July 1796, aged only 37.

Although his reputation as a poet was already well established, he was first buried in a modest grave in the north-west corner of St. Michael's churchyard. In 1815, however, his remains were transferred to a new mausoleum which had been erected in his memory.

Burns's widow continued to live in the house in Dumfries with her family until her own death in 1834. The house soon became a place of pilgrimage for the many tourists - William Wordsworth among them - who wished to pay their respects to the poet's memory.

Many sites associated with Burns can be seen, and form part of the BURNS HERITAGE TRAIL.

ROBERT BURNS CENTRE Mill Road, Dumfries. A recent addition to the Burns Heritage Trail and an absorbing introduction to the life of Burns and the busy and lively Dumfries of the 1790s. The new centre is housed in an attractive C18th sandstone mill on the banks of the Nith, not far from the town centre. Exhibits on Burns's- life in Dumfries are supplemented by an audio-visual presentation 'Robert Burns, The Dumfries Years' and 'Dumfries, Queen of the South'. The exhibition gallery contains many original manuscripts and relics of the poet and a scale model of the town. On the first floor is Jean Armour's Pantry, a luxurious cafe with window seating and, for sunny days, picnic benches overlooking the river and caul. The centre also provides space for temporary exhibitions and the foyer contains a book shop and information desk. In the evening the centre shows a wide range of quality feature films, not usually available outside large cities and is a major cultural asset to south-west Scotland, aided financially by the Scottish Film Council.

BURNS HOUSE Burns Street. This was Burns's home from May 1793 till his death in July 1796. Furnished in the style of the period, it contains many relics associated with the poet and his life.

BURNS MAUSOLEUM St. Michael's churchyard. This elaborate monument was not built until nearly 20 years after his death.

THE GLOBE INN Off the High Street, Dumfries. One of Burns's frequent haunts, 'my favourite howff', with his chair, an inscribed window pane and other relics, and the convivial atmosphere which he enjoyed.

ELLISLAND FARM Off A76, north of Dumfries. It was here that Burns wrote 'Auld Lang Syne' and one of his best known poems 'Tam O'Shanter'. The granary contains a display of Burns's life as a farmer, and his attempts to improve the land. There is a riverside walk.

You can also seek out other places associated with Burns, such as the river quays at KINGHOLM and GLENCAPLE on B725, south of Dumfries. Further west you can find The Selkirk Arms in KIRKCUDBRIGHT, where he wrote the noted 'Selkirk Grace', or the Murray Arms Hotel in GATEHOUSE-OF-FLEET where he composed the famous lines 'Scots Wha Hae'. You can also visit the ancient iron-rich mineral spring at BROW WELL, west of Ruthwell on B725, sought out by Burns in an attempt to cure his final illness.

The coastal area between Criffel Hill in the east and Cairnharrow Hill in the west is intersected by three estuaries. In the centre is the River Dee with the town of Kirkcudbright at the head of the estuary; to the east the Water of Urr flows into the Solway past the town of Dalbeattie; to the west the Water of Fleet flows through the beautiful Fleet Bay, with Gatehouse-of-Fleet the main town of the district. These two latter estuaries have been classified as National Scenic Areas, one known as the Fleet Valley, the other as the East Stewartry Coast, which includes Auchencairn Bay, Orchardton Bay, Rough Firth, Sandyhills Bay and the Mersehead Sands.

The area around Kirkcudbright is known as the Stewartry. It was at one time the property of the powerful Balliols but, owing to that family's uncertain loyalty, it was taken from them by the king, who then appointed a steward to hold jurisdiction over it. This office was, in fact, held by the Maxwell family for many generations.

The capital of the Stewartry is Kirkcudbright. This has long been an important gateway to the sea, and is still used as such today. Visitors will enjoy looking at the picturesque old harbour with its white painted houses, where fishing boats still tie up. The local sea-food, too, is well worth tasting. It is surprising to find, in the centre of the town, a huge tower house of the C16th, MacLellan's Castle, now a substantial ruin. The old market cross, dating from 1610, still stands, and so does the ancient Tolbooth, still with its 'jougs', a kind of iron manacle to which wrongdoers could be fastened to receive public beatings. These would not only be thieves and minor criminals, but also people suspected of heresy or witchcraft.

Much of Kirkcudbright has wide C18th streets and delightful houses painted in shades of pink, blue, cream, green and buff, with the windows often in white or a contrasting colour, giving a light and spacious air which, together with the numerous flower beds, contrast somewhat incongruously with the forbidding tower house.

This is a pleasant town which invites the visitor to linger; to discover picturesque corners to photograph; to browse among the shops, selling knitwear and gifts, antiques and small collectable items, or gourmet foods from the local area; to seek out the different craft workers and artists in the district. This town has been a popular place for artists to live, their numbers including E.A.Hornel whose old home is open to the public. Another place of interest is the Stewartry Museum, with a wealth of information about the district. Robert Burns wrote his 'Selkirk Grace' in an inn here, and lovers of detective fiction can trace Dorothy Sayers' 'Five red Herrings' round the area, for she knew the town well. There are, of course, opportunities for fishing, while sea-angling is becoming a very popular pursuit, and there is a good 18-hole golf course. Tours of the nearby Tongland Power Station can be arranged. This is a lively and friendly town, where the Kirkcudbright Summer Festivities run for several weeks, offering enjoyment to local people and to visitors alike.

Burns is reputed to have written 'Scots wha hae' in Gatehouse-of-Fleet, along the coast to the west. This town, originally planned as a centre of commerce, and retaining the well laid out streets and spacious air of the C18th, is also popular with visitors, lying, as it does, in the beautiful Fleet Valley. THis is a long established, prosperous and well wooded district, with the forbidding Cardoness Castle as a reminder of more turbulent days. Visitors need only walk up a small field, Venniehill, the property of the National Trust for Scotland and just off the main street of Gatehouse-of-Fleet to be rewarded with a marvellous view of the rich and varied countryside. Nearby the Fleet Oakwoods Interpretive Trail takes you through fine broad-leaved woodland, with the Murray Forest Centre to tell you about the management of such woodlands, and there are many other delightful walks in the area.

This coast is also very popular, for there are sandy beaches with safe bathing between rocky points, and at Brighouse Bay sailing, water sports, riding and pony trekking. The coast to the east of Kirkcudbright is equally attractive, though until you reach Dundrennan much of the part south of the A711 is reserved as a military training area. The East Stewartry National Scenic Area encompasses much of the coastline south of Dalbeattie.

Dalbeattie itself is a complete contrast to Kirkcudbright. In the last century vast amounts of granite were shipped from here and much of the town dates from that time, with sturdy rows of one or two storey houses and solidly built public buildings. Much of the town is built of this granite and the unpainted stones of the buildings, grey on a wet day, sparkle with tiny specks of light as soon as the sun shines, giving it a very cheerful atmosphere. Besides a pleasant park, with bandstand and boating lake the town has Dalbeattie Forest on the outskirts where it is possible to walk and picnic.

This is a beautiful coast of immense variety, with inlets, estuaries and bays between rocky headlands contrasting with the wide expanse of the Mersehead Sands, and the National Trust for Scotland owns several places in the area. Here you can find rocky headlands, small inlets and harbours, and coves of sand and rocks, or, if you prefer, wide beaches and miles of sand backed by dunes or by low-lying salt marshes and flat pastureland. In many places the hills inland are well wooded and the mixed forestry and farming lies in pleasant contrast to the open sea, while there are magnificent views over the Solway Firth to the Mountains of the Lake District and the Cumbrian coast. It is an ever changing scene, for bays which are immense expanses of sand glinting with channels of water will, in a few hours' time, be completely covered by the sea, the waves lapping against the shoreline, and boats which were formerly lying tilted to one side on mud will be riding high again on blue water.

Settlement has been long established here. Cairnholy Chambered Cairns, constructed by early neolithic man, are just beyond Gatehouse-of-Fleet; the Mote of Mark was once an Iron Age hill-fort; the great abbey at Dundrennan dates from the C12th; the tower houses at Orchardton and Cardoness recall the troubled times of the C15th, while Cally House and Arbigland are mansions constructed by wealthy men of the peaceful C18th. There are beautiful gardens, too, to enjoy at Arbigland, and these are open some days each week in summer. There are many other gardens, too, which may be visited occasionally under Scotland's Gardens Scheme, with the proceeds going to charitable causes.

It was during the reign of Queen Victoria that this coast first became popular for recreation and leisure, the 'Scottish Riviera' as it was called on account of the mild climate, seaside coves, trees and flowers. Now, with more than a century of providing for holiday-makers, it can offer every facility to the visitor. You can choose to stay in a luxury hotel or a family-run guest house, a village pub or a bed-and-breakfast home; there are former Victorian villas or modern log cabins to rent; there are numerous camp sites, many with spectacular views over the sea, with facilities for both caravans and tents. There are sandy beaches for children to play on, with parking nearby, often with facilities for the disabled, and rocky coves to explore. For the most part bathing is possible only at high tide and swimming far out is not advised where fast

tides sweep round the headlands. In places the sea ebbs far over the sands and it is unsafe ever to walk out to meet the oncoming tide, for the water flows in through channels hardly noticeable to people who do not know the coast, coming very much faster than might be expected, and cutting off all possible retreat.

In summer brightly coloured boats add to the gaiety of the scene, for sailing is a pastime growing in popularity every year. There are full launching and mooring facilities at Kippford and the yacht club here organises races in which visitors are welcome to compete. If you are not an expert there are places where you can learn to sail, or just take a boat trip with someone else to do the work. There is plenty of choice for fishermen, sea angling from Kirkcudbright or Kippford, game or coarse fishing in rivers or on small lochs, and the naturalist will enjoy the variety of bird life to be seen, Rough Island being a noted breeding ground for sea birds. Walkers may choose a coastal path one day, and the next go deep into a forest. There is riding to be enjoyed and for golfers several courses to choose from, including a championship one at Southerness.

A succession of Festivals provide entertainment throughout the summer. The Galloway Arts Festival is spread through many locations, with exhibitions of art and of craftwork, concerts, theatrical productions and puppets. In addition to the annual festivities at Kirkcudbright and Dalbeattie, the Kippford Regatta is a colourful occasion, and the World Flounder Tramping Championship at Palnackie a time of fun for competitors and spectators alike.

Pleasant locations and good custom from the many visitors have encouraged a number of craft workers to set up studios or workshops in the area. Kirkcudbright, as has been mentioned, has long been a favourite with artists, and crafts of diverse kinds, jewellery, glass blowing or engraving, pottery and modelling will be found in various places along the coast, with a number now in the Palnackie area, as well as in Kirkcudbright and Gatehouse-of-Fleet.

Although quiet walks and picnic areas can be discovered, especially inland, the coast is a busy and lively place, with every facility for the visitor, many welcomes for children, friendly pubs and restaurants, camping sites, seaside walks, golf, sands and sailing, all making an enjoyable holiday in the mild climate and invigorating sea air, with something for everyone to enjoy, old or young.

At the heart of Dumfries and Galloway is the region known as the Glenkens. This is the upper part of the valley, once a series of narrow lochs, from which the river Dee flows into the sea at Kirkcudbright. The water level in these lochs was raised to provide power for the hydro electric scheme in the 1930s and the enlarged Loch Ken is now a significant feature of the valley. Near to the southern end is Castle Douglas. This is a planned town, founded in the late C18th by Sir William Douglas, a merchant who had made a fortune in Virginia and the West Indies and wished to establish a centre of commerce in his native Galloway.

Castle Douglas was laid out with three parallel streets, wide and commodious. Although Sir William's original idea of establishing the cotton industry here was not in the long term successful, the town soon became an important market, with cattle and horse fairs, and has remained a thriving centre for the prosperous local farming area, the home of the annual Stewartry Agricultural Show and of the Dumfries and Galloway Horse Show, and with an auction mart, one of the most modern in Scotland, disposing of over £17 million worth of stock in a year.

Beside the town is the beautiful Carlingwark Loch, dotted with islands, where visitors can enjoy boating and picnicking, or learn to sail. At the far end of the loch are Threave Gardens, the teaching garden of the National Trust for Scotland, which is open to visitors all year. On the other side of the A75 road is Threave Castle on an island in the river Dee, the great fortress of the Douglases, which can be reached by ferry. Nearby, also, is Threave Wildfowl Refuge, for this area is an important place for wintering wildfowl, where visitors may watch the birds from hides during the winter months.

The A713 road runs north from Castle Douglas toward Ayr, and is a noted Galloway Tourist Route, marked with road signs bearing a white thistle on a brown background. This follows the eastern shore of the loch with good views over the water. Clustered close together at the head of the loch are New Galloway, St. John's Town of Dalry and Balmaclellan. Here the road crosses the river and continues past further lochs and then over moorland to Carsphairn.

The hydro-electric scheme was built between 1931 and 1935, and all the lochs in the valley, as well as Loch Doon to the north and the specially created loch of Clatteringshaws, are connected, some by means of tunnels, with the main station at Tongland near Kirkcudbright. St. John's Town of Dalry got its name from the Knights of St. John, a military order originally founded to assist pilgrims on the way to Jerusalem. Dalry was on the route taken by pilgrims from Edinburgh and the north to Whithorn, and many, including kings and queens, stopped here on their journeys. New Galloway was founded later, in 1633, by Viscount Kenmure. It did not immediately prosper and has remained Scotland's smallest royal burgh.

This area was the source of the Pentland Rising in 1666, when a large body of Covenanters marched on Edinburgh, only to be defeated by much more powerful government forces. There are many associations with Covenanters, including a statue of Robert Paterson, who cut many of the long inscriptions on their tombstones.

Active people will find a great deal of enjoyment in this district. The Southern Upland Way passes through Dalry, and there are many other hill walks in the rugged country which will appeal to the serious walker, as well as easier strolls and picnic sites for the less ambitious.

Loch Ken has been developed carefully for recreation and now has a wide range of sports, with special areas reserved for certain activities. Rowing boats can be beached or moored, and there are a number of moorings for sailing dinghies. If you are a complete novice you can learn to sail at the Galloway Sailing Centre on the eastern shore. The centre of the loch has an area where water ski-ing is permitted, and has become a well-established place for this sport, with visitors coming from all over Britain. Power boats are restricted to certain areas, where they can enjoy thier sport without causing any annoyance to other users of the loch.

It is hardly necessary to say that fishing is available, including game fishing for salmon, grilse and sea-trout, and also coarse fishing, particularly of pike. The loch is also of great interest to bird watchers, with habitats ranging from broad-leaved woodland to reed-beds, and wildfowl include geese, whooper swans, ducks and the great crested grebe. Thre are also facilities for pony-trekking, an ideal way to see the countryside.

The road from New Galloway to Newton Stewart passes through the Galloway Forest Park and visitors can enjoy the Deer Museum, the Red Deer Range, the Wild Goat Park, see Clydesdale horses at work, or take the Raiders Road Forest Drive, which has special picnic areas.

Newton Stewart lies just south of the junction of the Penkiln Burn and the river Cree, the town being picturesquely sited on the slopes rising from the river. Across the river from Newton Stewart is Minnigaff, which is, in fact, the older settlement, though today much smaller than Newton Stewart. There are traces of a former motte at Minnigaff and the village lay on the old road followed by travellers, and especially pilgrims, on their way to Whithorn, so that in medieval days this was a useful stopping place, and also provided an important market for the people of the surrounding hills.

It was not until the C17th that Newton Stewart was developed by William Stewart, but this eventually became the more important centre. An attempt was later made by Sir William Douglas to set up a cotton industry here as at Castle Douglas (and change the name to Newton Douglas) but the venture did not prosper. Newton Stewart, however, does have a very successful industry in the weaving of wool, mohair being a speciality, and it is possible for visitors to make a tour of some mills. Today this is a busy but not overlarge town, with a pleasant mixture of building styles and materials, and with a fine bridge over the river by John Rennie, built in 1813. There is a museum with old implements used in the district and a display of dresses and shawls.

Newton Stewart is within reach of the coast, of the forest and of mountains, and some of Galloway's finest scenery is to be found here. To the east of the town is Cairnsmore of Fleet, rising steeply to 711m (2331ft), the mountain round which Richard Hannay was pursued in John Buchan's 'The Thirty-nine Steps', while to the north is the Merrick, at 840m (2766ft) the highest mountain in Southern Scotland, together with several other summits of more than 610m (2000ft). The Merrick can be climbed by starting from Bruce's Stone in Glen Trool. Dividing the district from the Glenkens is another range, the Rhinns of Kells, with four summits over 610m (2000ft).

There are many associations here with Robert Bruce, for the Carrick, to the north and once part of Galloway, was his homeland, and it was at Loch Trool that he scored his first victory over an English army, an event which set him on the road to his final triumph at Bannockburn seven years later. Another victory is commemorated by a stone near the road from Newton Stewart to New Galloway.

The Southern Upland Way crosses the country, and although much of it is demanding walking the section along Glen Trool is relatively easy and can be enjoyed by less experienced walkers. Glen Trool is a favourite place to visit and is well provided with signposted trails and picnic places, and also has facilities for the disabled. The loch, long and narrow, with craggy hillsides, a mixture of deciduous and coniferous trees and tumbling waterfalls is reminiscent of Highland scenery.

Much of the area is within the Galloway Forest Park, but do not imagine that this means it is entirely covered by conifers. Some parts, such as the Merrick, are too high and exposed to be planted, while in other places areas have been left unplanted, or trees cleared to open up a particularly fine view. Nor is the forest without deciduous trees, and at Glen Trool remnants of the ancient forest cover of oak, alder, birch and hazel add colour to the scene, particularly in spring and autumn. The Forest has a number of picnic areas, and special attractions are to be found by the Queen's Way, the A712 road from Newton Stewart to New Galloway, including the Deer Museum, the Red Deer Range, The Wild Goat Park and a special forest drive open in summer, the Raiders Road, with picnic places along the way. There are forest trails, too, close to Newton Stewart at Kirroughtree Forest, where there is a visitor centre, a bird trail and a forest garden. There are many easy pleasant walks in this area, by the Penkiln Burn and also up the Palnure Burn, with another forest picnic area close by.

It is by no means only forest and hills which attract the visitor to Newton Stewart, for the A75 road toward Gatehouse-of-Fleet runs along the coast and is considered to be one of the most beautiful drives in the south of Scotland. On this stretch of coast is Creetown, not only in a beautiful situation but also the home of the Gem Rock Museum, which no visitor should miss, and of the well-known silversmith, John Prince. Along this stretch of coast, too, are the Cairnholy Chambered Cairns, built by neolithic man, who evidently shared all our liking for a good view, and the C16th Carsluith Castle. The beach along here is mainly shingle but you will find some attractive sandy coves at Mossyard Bay beyond the headland, where the A75 leaves the coast.

The Cree is the best known salmon river in Galloway, and visitors will see stake nets in the estuary and will be able to purchase delicious home smoked salmon in the locality. Beats to fish on the river are much sought after, and this area is well known to many fishermen.

The Anwoth Hotel

Gatehouse of Fleet, Castle Douglas, Kirkcudbrightshire.
Tel: (05574) 217

Delightful country hotel family run with excellent food and comfortable accommodation which includes 6 bedrooms, one being a family room, some en suite, all with tea/coffee making facilities. The hotel offers 2 bars and there is a delightful garden with river.

We are open all day and non residents are welcome.

We offer an ideal base for your holiday so give us a ring for the tariff or just pop in and try our excellent meals.

Monreith Arms Hotel

Port William
Wigtownshire
DG8 9SE

Come and fish, relax, or even play free golf at two golf courses!

For excellent Salmon & Trout – on the Rivers Cree and Bladnoch. Local Loch fishing & private water fishing can be arranged between June & September!

Comfortable, friendly accommodation with bars, lounge, and A`La Carte restaurant.

Reduced rates for mid-week breaks, long weekends and groups of 10 or more.

**For further details
Telephone: 09887 232**

Driving along the A75, it is easy to miss out this peninsula, without turning to explore it. This would be a pity for its landscape is unusual and it contains many of the most interesting relics of Galloway's history. Today it seems isolated, when the main road hurries past to Stranraer, touching only the north-west corner and Glenluce. But this was not the case when transport by land was difficult and travel by sea common.

The neolithic people came to this country by boat, leaving evidence of their presence along sea coasts from the Mediterranean to Scotland. Without iron tools to clear heavily wooded inland areas, they often chose to remain on the lighter soils of hilly districts, and they and their successors of the Bronze Age have left numerous burial cairns, standing stones and marked rocks, as a glance at an Ordnance Survey map will show, throughout this peninsula and north of Glenluce. Outstanding among them are the Torhousekie Stone Circle, one of the best preserved of the kind in Britain, and the Standing Stones and Cup-and-Ring Markings at Drumtroddan. Rispain Camp and Barsalloch Fort date from the Iron Age, a time when defence was of primary importance.

It was by sea, too, that St. Ninian came to the country, to found the first Christian church at Whithorn, where excavations are drawing increasing numbers of visitors. Archaeological discoveries were made on a site intended for sheltered housing in 1984, and these were of such great interest that the dig was extended, becoming one of the largest in Europe. Visitors will be fascinated by the work, which is carefully explained for them. The Isle of Whithorn and Chapel Finian were landing places for pilgrims, and a network of paths to create a modern 'pilgrim's way' will link up with the Southern Upland Way. The museum contains exceptionally early Christian crosses.

Norman remains, too, are found in the church at Cruggleton and in the exceptional Druchtag Motte, while the Middle Ages saw the building of the Abbey at Glenluce and a constant stream of pilgrims to the shrine of St. Ninian and the Priory at Whithorn. The imposing tower houses of Castle of Park and the Old Place of Mochrum recall the turbulent C16th, and the troubled days of the Covenanters are remembered by the memorials at Wigtown to the two women drowned there, an infamous deed, always quoted as the epitome of the 'Killing Times'.

The more peaceful C18th and C19th still saw the peninsula as essential to trade. Garlieston was founded about 1760 by Lord Garlies for ship-building and the import of heavy goods, while on the opposite side of the peninsula Sir William Maxwell founded Port William. Railways once ran both to Whithorn and to Garlieston.

Wigtown had long been the capital of the region, having been given the status of a royal burgh by 1292, with a busy medieval harbour, a castle and a priory. It remained an important harbour, with quays along the river Bladnoch, until the early years of this century when many channels were blocked by silt. To realise how the sea has retreated, look at the stake to which the two martyrs were tied, in a place where it would now be totally impossible for anyone to drown. The large square in the centre of the town, with the houses painted in different colours and two market crosses, is typical of the unhurried and friendly atmosphere of the region. For interesting places to go, you can choose between a martyrs' memorial on a hilltop with magnificent views, a tour of a whisky distillery at Bladnoch, a bird garden with tropical birds, or, not far away, the Torhousekie stone circle.

Much of the country is fertile farmland and rolling hills, but anyone who drives from Wigtown to Whithorn and Port William will notice how the scenery changes from the sheltered eastern and northern part, with fine trees and hedges, to the stony fields and gorse of the exposed south-western coast. To the north-west are moorland and lochs, on one of which is a rare inland cormorant colony.

The area has much to offer the holiday maker as well as antiquities. Some of the finest cliff scenery of the whole Galloway coast is to be found at the exposed Burrow Head, while, in contrast, sandy beaches can be enjoyed at Monreith Bay. This area is well used to visitors and is provided with hotels, camp sites and picnic places. Boats can be launched from slipways at Isle of Whithorn and Port William, and the small harbours are popular with yachtsmen and also provide opportunities for sea-angling. Golfers can compare the 9-hole parkland course at Wigtown with the links at Port William, or try a round on the 18-hole course at Glenluce, the finest links course in the south of Scotland.

With none of the land far from the sea, the climate is mild and on the sheltered eastern coast are the gardens of Galloway House, first planted in the C18th, and open to visitors, while the gardens of Glenwhan and Castle Kennedy are not far from Glenluce.

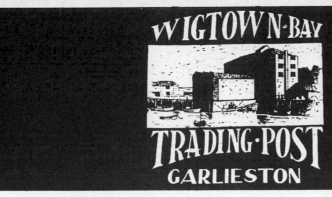

The Rhins is the name of the hammerheaded peninsula at the western extremity of Dumfries and Galloway, with its tip running down to Scotland's most southerly point. This district has always had important connections with Ireland, and today is a major link for travellers, cars and freight. Ferry services run from Stranraer and Cairnryan, both on the shores of the sheltered Loch Ryan.

Stranraer is an old settlement, with a castle dating from the C16th, and in the C18th and C19th was a busy shipping centre, with ship-building in addition. It was not the main ferry port for Ireland in the days when sailing ships had to change course and negotiate the length of Loch Ryan, but with the coming of steam, the advantages of the sheltered Loch outweighed the shorter crossing from the more exposed Portpatrick. The Stranraer-Larne route opened in 1872, and is now carrying an increasing volume of traffic, with a large complex of modern port facilities. Cairnryan was a military port during the last war but now caters also for the ferry traffic.

Although Loch Ryan is no longer needed, the Ministry of Defence has retained some land at the head of Luce Bay,with restricted access, and there is an RAF airfield nearby.

The A75 road, with huge vehicles carrying freight to and from Ireland, is busy and noisy but passes through only a small section of the town. Away from the port are comfortable hotels and friendly guest houses, camping and caravan sites. There are gardens where you can sit among flowers and watch the ships going in and out of the busy harbour, parks where children can play safely, and a splendid golf course designed by the late James Braid and used for championship matches. Stranraer is the location for the Galloway Games, with trials of strength, music and dancing traditionally associated with the Highlands, as well as Agricultural and Horticultural Shows.

The Rhins has a long history of settlement, with traces of ancient cairns, forts, mottes, the only broch in this part of Scotland, and the very early Christian stones at Kirkmadrine, dating back to the C5th. Later times have left us Stranraer Castle, Lochnaw Castle, and the remains of Dunskey Castle, near Portpatrick, in a spectacular setting.

For many years, Portpatrick, with the short crossing to Donaghadee, was the main port for travellers to Ireland, until the coming of steam packet-boats. It still has its most picturesque old harbour with its rocky entrance and is still busy with small trawlers, yachts and boats. The old round church tower probably served as a beacon for ships in the C17th, and the harbour was rebuilt more than once in an effort to enlarge it and make it more sheltered, but the sea always proved too stormy, and when the mail steamers moved to Stranraer further attempts were abandoned. The place is a favourite with holiday-makers, its charm recognised long ago by the building, in 1902, of a majestic hotel in the then fashionable Scottish Baronial style. Visitors can enjoy a park, a playground, a small beach, and opportunities for walks, including the first part of the Southern Upland Way along the coast. Sailors and sea-anglers use the harbour, while golfers have two courses to choose from. People will also enjoy a visit to 'Little Wheels' the Lifeboat Exhibition and the various craft shops.

Further south along the coast is Port Logan. Although this never achieved the success of Port Patrick it is a delightful place with a small old lighthouse and a line of houses around a sandy bay. Here is the unique Logan Fish Pond, and nearby is the Famous Logan Botanic Garden, an outpost of the Royal Botanic Garden in Edinburgh, where the exceptional mildness of the climate enables even palm trees to grow outside. There are three other outstanding gardens in the area, at Ardwell, and at Castle Kennedy and Glenwhan.

Families with young children will probably be looking for sandy beaches, and these will be found on the sheltered eastern side of the peninsula, with the village of Sandhead a central point with long stretches of golden sand, and a number of other bays at New England, Drummore and Maryport. Those who prefer dramatic cliff scenery will find it along the exposed western seaboard, though even here some sandy bays are found. On this rocky exposed coast there are working lighthouses at the Mull of Galloway, Killantringan and Corsewall, and also one at Cairn Point in Loch Ryan. The Mull of Galloway is a popular expedition, the 'Land's End' of Scotland, surrounded by cliffs and a notable haunt of sea-birds. Visitors who enjoy an active holiday will find opportunities for sailing, boating and water-skiing at Loch Ryan, as well as ridng and golf. Portpatrick provides sea-angling and facilities for yachts. If you don't want to do the hard work yourself you can be taken on a voyage round the Western Isles, or go on one of the numerous and very comfortable ferries to Ireland just for a day trip.

The Logan Botanic Garden is a walled garden near Portlogan, off the B7065, 14 miles south of Stranraer in south-west Scotland and is famous for its rare exotic plants, ferns, cabbage palms and Australian gums.

Open daily 10 a.m.-5 p.m. April to September inclusive.
Admission: Cars and Passengers 70p.
No animals. Refreshment facilities available.

Outdoor Activities

This district has something to offer the active of all ages, from a three-year-old on the beach to a ninety-year-old enjoying a game of bowls on one of the many greens, and of all tastes, whether you are a water-skiing or wind-surfing enthusiast or prefer to sit quietly in a boat trailing a fishing line in the sea.

There are many challenging walks, including the first part of the Southern Upland Way - if you are a bit doubtful of your capabilities, it is possible to follow this route with an experienced guide and safari landrover support. Guided hill walks can be found in the Moffat area, and there are a number of way-marked walks from Carsphairn, high in the uplands. You can enjoy guided walks, too, in the less demanding Wigtownshire district, or, if you prefer, acquire a series of leaflets which will direct you round the interesting sites. There is a wealth of way-marked walks and trails through the Forests, some taking all or half a day, some little more than strolls, and the coast, also, has way-marked walks, including the beautiful Jubilee path by the Colvend coast or the first part of the Southern Upland Way from Portpatrick.

Golf has from old times been known in Scotland as 'the Royal and Ancient Game' so it is not surprising that the area has no fewer than 23 golf courses. There is the fine course designed by James Braid at Stranraer, or the natural links at Southerness, both of them used for championship matches. There are other 18-hole courses, too, at all the larger centres. But if you are just a holiday-maker with modest ambitions, or someone who may be an expert but would like to try out a lot of different places, there are many 9-hole courses, some parkland and some links, most of them with majestic views to enjoy as well as providing an interesting game. If you feel rather less energetic, there is often a putting green to be found in the local park, and bowling is a popular pursuit here, with a large number of greens. A number of parks, too, have public tennis courts. If you are a winter visitor, possibly having come to see the bird life, you may also enjoy curling, another popular Scottish game, on the ice rink at Lockerbie.

Dumfries and Galloway has long been known for the quality of its fishing. It is not only the large rivers of the main valleys which are noted for their salmon and sea-trout, but these fish may be taken in many other smaller waters or in some lochs. The best stretches of rivers will be booked well in advance or may be taken from year to year, so people who wish to pursue this sport should consult the Tourist Information Centre before their holiday, or the local Angling Associations, who are always very helpful. Some hotels may include the right to fish in a stay at the hotel, the Warmanbie Hotel at Annan, for instance, which is set in wooded grounds overlooking the river, has the right to fish one rod on a good stretch of this famous salmon river, and a fisherman staying there will be able to have his fishing free, an ideal way to spend a holiday.

As well as salmon and sea-trout there are numerous places with brown trout or rainbow. The Galloway Forest Park includes a number of streams and lochs, on some of which boats are available, and a 17lb brown trout has been taken in Loch Doon. There are a number of stocked lochs, with brown and rainbow trout, for fly-fishing only, and an angling centre at Moffat offers tuition, so that you can try your hand at this difficult art - you can even hire the equipment and discover if this is the sport for you without committing yourself to great expense. Coarse fishing is one of the most popular pastimes in the British Isles, and here again there is a wealth of opportunity. Carp, bream, tench and roach are to be found in many lochs. Lochmaben, Castle Douglas and Dalbeattie are particularly good places to take children who want to fish. If you want something large to show off, try Loch Ken - pike up to 70lbs have been caught there.

If you are really after monsters, then you will want to try sea-angling. Tope and shark have been landed by anglers from Isle of Whithorn, and boats from Portpatrick, Kippford and Kirkcudbright regularly set out to sea for angling trips. You do not need, of course, to go on a boat, for there are many places along the coast where you can fish from rocks by the shore. Loch Ryan, Isle of Whithorn and Kirkcudbright have sea-angling Open Shore Festivals and championships.

The sea is an endless source of entertainment with many sandy beaches where children will enjoy playing. It must be remembered that the tide recedes far over the sands of the Solway Firth and here bathing and paddling are possible only at high tide. The most easterly shores, also, are swept by very fast tides and swimming is not advisable. The local Tourist Information Centre provides a list of sandy beaches, with information about their safety, as well as parking and toilet facilities.

There are, of course, swimming pools, one at Dumfries open all year, and others which are open daily during the holidays but will have some restrictions on use during term time. Many hotels have their own swimming pools; one luxury hotel even has an outdoor heated pool.

There is plenty of choice for yachtsmen, with Kippford the headquarters of the Solway Yacht Club and many harbours along the coast, including Kirkcudbright, where yachts can put in. Garlieston and Port William were founded originally for commercial traffic in the C18th but are now quiet places which make interesting ports of call. Yachting is now the main pastime at Isle of Whithorn, once a landing place for pilgrims, and Portpatrick, formerly the ferry port for Ireland, is able to accommodate ocean-going yachts. If you are not a boat owner yourself you can charter a boat, either to sail yo urself or, if you are not experienced, under the guidance of a friendly skipper.

For sailing in the Solway, it is necessary to have a knowledge and understanding of tides. If you are not accustomed to the sea, you may prefer sailing on an inland loch. There are facilities for boating and for sailing small boats at Lochmaben and on Carlingwark Loch near Castle Douglas. The main place in the region, however, is Loch Ken, which has been developed as a water sports and recreation centre. Loch Ken is a long loch, and there are several places with moorings for sailing dinghies, as well as others where rowing boats can be moored or beached. You can also spend a very enjoyable holiday and feel you have accomplished something by learning to sail, or by improving your technique. The Galloway Sailing Centre, recognised by the Royal Yachting Association, runs courses for sailors of all standards and ages who want to go for the R.Y.A. awards, with friendly and encouraging instructors. People who just want to 'mess about in boats' will find a great selection of sailing dinghies, windsurfers and canoes for less formal instruction or just for hire. The facilities at the club are open to everyone and would be hard to beat at most yacht clubs, and yet the prices remain very competitive. As well as sailing, rowing, canoeing and wind-surfing, a part of the lake is designated for power boating and water-skiing, and Loch Ken has become a recognised centre for this demanding sport. Water-skiing is also available in Loch Ryan.

For centuries people have bred and ridden horses in Galloway, and there are many opportunities for pony-trekking, now becoming a favourite way of seeing the country. Riding experience is not necessary, for you need do little more than sit on a well-mannered and sure-footed pony, in a party always led by an experienced rider. If you want to do serious riding you will find facilities for that as well, with a number of riding stables, a centre at Moffat with horses for all ages, even small children, and an equitation centre near Dumfries with an indoor riding school. The variety of country, fields and forests make hacking particularly enjoyable here.

Riding horses is not the only way to get about. Remember that Kirkpatrick Macmillan invented the bicycle here and think of a cycling holiday, one of the best of all ways to explore the country and get to know the people on your way, rather than rushing past in a car. There is a network of quiet country roads, the hills are not too punishing, and the scenery is exceptional. The Tourist Information Centre produces a leaflet with suggested routes that cyclists will enjoy - even if you don't emulate the inventor and cycle to Glasgow. Because of its history, the region has a very warm welcome for cyclists, both modern machine and veteran enthusiasts, who will find many special events, rallies and races to take part in.

A growing enthusiasm in recent years has been for holiday parks, where you can participate in a whole variety of sports, all laid on for you to enjoy without any difficulty. A typical holiday park is found at Brighouse Bay, where day visitors are welcome to use the facilities. Here you can hire a bicycle, or go pony-trekking on a sturdy Highland pony. Experienced riders can go hacking. Children are welcome, and encouraged to groom and feed their ponies. You can learn to sail or, if you are experienced, hire a sailing dinghy for a day. Canoeing is available, and this might be your opportunity to learn wind-surfing or water-skiing. You can hire a rowing boat to go fishing in the bay or take part in a sea-angling contest from the rocks by the shore. Children love the mini-golf and the pedal boats on the pond, and nature lovers can join a walk with a Nature Conservancy Officer. Regular farm tours are organised. Holiday Parks are perticularly good for family holidays, with entertainment for children, their parents, and grandma and grandpa as well.

In the more prestigious price bracket, there are hotels, sometimes on the estates of former mansions, which can provide their guests with salmon fishing, rough shooting, roe deer stalking, or riding, in addition to their own swimming pool, bowling green and tennis courts, and sometimes even a heli-pad!

This drive explores the country north of Dumfries, from the fertile Nith valley to the bare Lowther Hills, from a miner's cottage to a nobleman's castle. (74 miles, 119km, not counting short detours for visits)

Leave Dumfries by A76, signposted Kilmarnock. Soon a sign indicates **Lincluden College** on your right. If you visit the college, return to A76. Just over 6 miles from Dumfries, you reach Robert Burns's farm at **Ellisland**. After a visit, return to A76. As you reach Carronbridge, there is a sign to the right, A702 to Durisdeer and Elvanfoot. Take this road. Within a few miles **Durisdeer** will be signposted on your right. After a visit to the church, return to A702 which now takes you through the dramatic **Dalveen Pass** and over the border into Strathclyde. Watch out for sheep and lambs on the unfenced road. Conifer plantations appear to your right. You reach Elvanfoot and here you should turn left on B7040, signposted Wanlockhead and The Scots Lead Mining Museum. The road goes over a beautiful expanse of carefully managed heather moorland. You reach Leadhills and here you turn left signposted Wanlockhead and the Lead Mining Museum. Continue along this road, marked further on as B797 to Sanquhar. You re-enter Dumfries and Galloway and reach **Wanlockhead**, a sign to the **Beam Engine** and the **Lead Mining Museum** to your right. The Visitor Centre is just below the main road. After your visit, return to A797 and continue as it winds down the **Mennock Pass** and out into woodland and fields to a junction with A76. Turn left for Dumfries here.

Good advance warning signs indicate a pleasant picnic area by the river on your right. Immediately beyond and almost next to the picnic area is a turn to the right. Turn right here over a bridge (This is a country road with beautiful views but if you wish to travel fast keep on A76 and follow signs for Drumlanrig). Follow this small road to a fork where a large sign to **Drumlanrig Castle** tells you to turn left. The road eventually goes over a cattle grid and you find yourself in the Castle parkland. At a T junction the Castle is to your right. On leaving follow the Castle drive to the main road. Do not cross the bridge but turn right, signposted Penpont. At a T junction (no signpost) turn right for **Penpont**. Beyond Penpont take the first left turn, signposted Dunscore and Dumfries, and a very small sign **Maxwelton**, the house being shortly on your right. At the next T junction go left and continue through **Dunscore** until the road joins A76 where you turn right for Dumfries.

This drive, starting from Castle Douglas, shows you something of the coast between Dalbeattie and Kirkcudbright, returning past the famous Threave Gardens. (55 miles, 88.5km)

Leave Castle Douglas by A745 for Dalbeattie. After some 5 miles you come to a junction. Turn left here and cross the bridge toward Dalbeattie. A short length of road brings you to the town sign. Do not go on but turn right here, signposted clearly Solway Coast.Almost immediately on your left is **Plantain Forest** picnic area. Continue along A710 to the sign for Kippford. Turn right to see **Kippford**. This attractive village on the estuary is at a dead end with limited parking space. You now have to return to A710. Further on a sign points right to **Rockcliffe**, which is also a dead end. There is a parking area above the village. Return to A710 and turn right, signposted Dumfries. You reach **Sandyhills** where there is a wide sandy beach, with parking. Turn left here on a road, opposite the beach car park, signposted to Barend and Dalbeattie. This joins a more major road where you go straight on for **Dalbeattie**. The road winds through the town and you then turn right at the T junction in the middle and shortly left, signposted Castle Douglas.

Retrace your route to cross the bridge again, but at the end keep left on A711 for Palnackie and Auchencairn. The road runs along level and fertile ground at the foot of the hills. You have to turn off left if you want to go into **Palnackie**, or to visit **Orchardton Tower**, signposted to the left, but return and continue on A711 through the village of **Auchencairn** and up the hill and on to **Dundrennan** where the impressive ruins of the abbey are by the roadside. Continue on A711 past the M.O.D restricted area and you find yourself with a wonderful view of the estuary. Continue into **Kirkcudbright**, a delightful town with C18th houses, an old harbour, old buildings and interesting museums. Leave Kirkcudbright by B727, which starts across the main street from MacLellan's Castle and is signposted Gelston. Follow the road up the hill, being careful to keep to the left round a steep corner still on B727, now signposted Dalbeattie. Follow this road through woodland and over moorland to Gelston. In the middle of the long straight village turn left, signposted Rhonehouse. At a crossroads do not go left for Rhonehouse but continue straight toward Castle Douglas. Round a bend **Threave Gardens**, belonging to the National Trust for Scotland, are on your left and **Carlingwark Loch** on your right. After visiting the gardens continue the short distance into Castle Douglas.

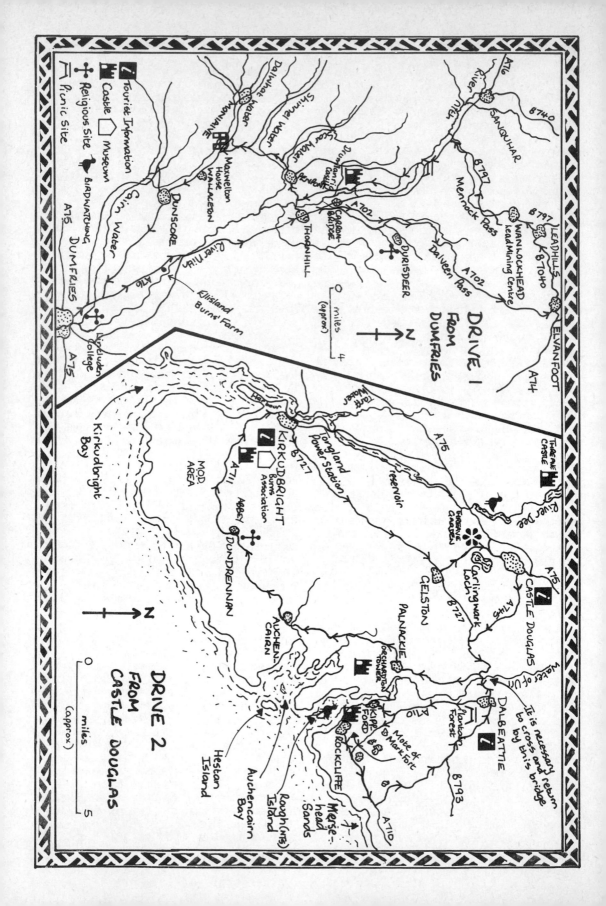

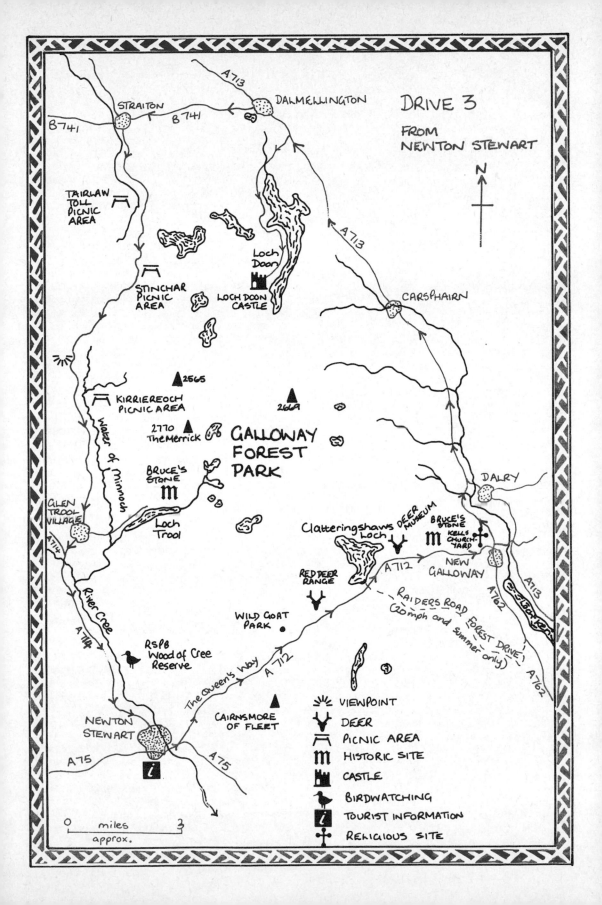

DRIVE 3

FROM
NEWTON STEWART

N

A713

STRAITON

B741

B741

DALMELLINGTON

TAIRLAW
TOLL
PICNIC
AREA

A713

STINCHAR
PICNIC
AREA

Loch
Doon

LOCH DOON CASTLE

CARSPHAIRN

2565

KIRRIEREOCH
PICNIC AREA

2669

Water of Minnoch

2770
The Merrick

GALLOWAY
FOREST
PARK

BRUCE'S
STONE
m

DALRY

GLEN
TROOL
VILLAGE

Loch
Trool

Clatteringshaws
Loch

DEER
MUSEUM

BRUCE'S
STONE
m

KELLS
CHURCHYARD

A714

RED DEER
RANGE

A712

NEW
GALLOWAY

A762

River Cree

A712

RAIDERS ROAD FOREST DRIVE
(20mph and summer only)

A713

A762

A714

WILD GOAT
PARK

RSPB
Wood of Cree
Reserve

The Queen's Way

A712

NEWTON
STEWART

CAIRNSMORE
OF FLEET

A75

i

A75

0   miles   3
approx.

☼ VIEWPOINT

Ⓨ DEER

⊓ PICNIC AREA

m HISTORIC SITE

🏰 CASTLE

🐦 BIRDWATCHING

i TOURIST INFORMATION

✝ RELIGIOUS SITE

This drive explores the magnificent inland scenery of the hills, and the extensive and beautiful Galloway Forest Park, starting from Newton Stewart. (This is a long drive, 80 miles, 129km, without counting the 14 mile, 22.5km, detour to Loch Doon, or the 8 mile, 13km, detour to Loch Trool. Taking the Raiders' Road Drive in place of A712 adds some 5 miles, 8km, to the tour).

Petrol is easily found in the towns and villages but motorists are warned that there are long stretches of road in the open country without filling stations.

Leave Newton Stewart on A75 in the direction of Dumfries. After 1 mile you turn off left on A712, signposted New Galloway and also Glentrool Forest Park. This is a magnificent drive, named the **Queen's Way** to celebrate the Silver Jubilee in 1977, with beautiful open views of Cairnsmore of Fleet. After some 5 miles look out for the **Wild Goat Park** signposted on the left. Shortly afterwards a signpost indicates the **Red Deer Range**. The road passes below the dam of Clatteringshaws Loch.

To your right is the start of the Raiders' Road Forest Drive, open only in summer. This is a forestry road and has a speed limit of 20 mph. Do not take this road now if you wish to see the Deer Museum and Bruce's Stone but continue on A712 and you will find the **Deer Museum** on the left and immediately afterwards the signpost to **Bruce's Stone**. If the **Raiders' Road** is open and you wish to take it, retrace your route and take the turn into the drive. If the drive is not open, continue along A712 to New Galloway.

If you reach **New Galloway** from A712, you have to turn right to see the town, the smallest royal burgh in Scotland. From the road junction clearly signposted at the north end of the town, take the A762 road toward Ayr. Almost immediately to your left is **Kells Churchyard** with interesting tombstones. Continue on A712 and cross the river at Earlston Power Station. The road now climbs slowly toward the hills until **Carsphairn** is reached. Keep on A713. This is a pass over barren moorland. A713 crosses the border into the Strathclyde Region and also the watershed, and descends a steep valley. After 2 miles a turning to the left is clearly signposted to **Loch Doon**. A little over 2 miles will take you to the near end of the loch, but the substantial ruins of the C14th castle are 7 miles from the A713 road. The road follows the gently sloping western shore of the long

loch, the opposite side well afforested. Afer the castle the road comes to an end and it is necessary to retrace the route to the A713. Continue your way on A713 to the sizable town of Dalmellington. The A713 road continues straight along one side of the town, without turning. Just beyond the end of the town turn left on to the clearly signposted B741 to Straiton. The Galloway Forest Park is also signposted. Watch out immediately for a very narrow hump-backed bridge. The road crosses a cattle grid, goes over more moorland and then, in complete contrast, descends into a sylvan landscape of green fields and trees set amongst the hills.

In **Straiton** turn left, clearly signposted for Newton Stewart and the Galloway Forest Park. Follow the road up the valley of the stream, until you reach a narrow bridge. Go over it carefully for at the end of it the road appears to sweep round to the left. But this much used roadway goes only to Bradan Treatment Works. The road you want is the insignificant one straight ahead, which has a very small signpost to Newton Stewart. You soon enter the Forest, with **Tairlaw Toll Picnic Area** on your right. The road then passes **Stinchar Picnic Area** and climbs gradually until the trees are left behind and it is crossing open ground where the summit of the pass is marked 1400 feet. Here the road is narrow with passing places, over moorland.

As you descend you come once more into well-grown forest, the trees blocking most of the view on either side until you reach the **Memorial** to David Bell, and it is well worth stopping here for the stupendous view of the mountains. At the road junction, keep left for Newton Stewart. You will pass **Kirrieroch Picnic Area** and then down on the low ground to your left **Palgowan Hill Farm**.

Well grown conifers now line the road on either side until the scene suddenly changes to deciduous trees and you are at Glentrool village. A well marked turning to the left here leads to **Glentrool**, a distance of four miles. Glentrool, with its rushing waterfall, long loch, trees and craggy hilltops is reminiscent of Highland scenery and is deservedly popular, with car parks and way-marked walks. **Bruce's Stone** commands a fine view. The road ends here and it is necessary to retrace the route to Glentrool village. Continue down the road from here to the junction with A714 and go left for Newton Stewart. This takes you alongside the beautiful Cree river, with the RSPB **Wood of Cree Reserve** signposted to the left and back into Newton Stewart.

Drives 4 and 5

This drive explores the varied scenery and the antiquities of the remote Machars region, starting from Wigtown. (51 miles, 82km)

Leave Wigtown by A746 to Whithorn (also marked A714). AT **Bladnoch** the distillery can be visited. A714 soon branches off and you continue on A746 to Kirkinner. Shortly after, take the left fork B7004 to Garlieston. You will arrive at a crossroads. To your left is the village of **Garlieston**. Opposite you is the entrance to **Galloway House Gardens** with a notice if they are open. They lie a mile down a narrow road with passing places. If you have visited the gardens return to the road and turn left (if not, turn right) still on B7004 which runs alongside the estate wall. Keep on this road, bearing left at the next junction, and stay on it, going right at the next fork, still B7004 to **Whithorn**. The Priory is in the centre of the village through a blue and white arch.

Leave Whithorn by a right fork at the end of the village, signposted Port William (A746). Soon **Rispain Camp** is on your left. When you reach a T junction with A747, turn right, signposted Port William. On this stretch of road you pass **Monreith Bay** and then **Barsalloch Fort** and follow along the shore to **Port William**. Here at a small roundabout, take A714 signposted Wigtown. In about 2 miles the road takes a sharp bend and shortly afterwards you pass the sign for **Drumtroddan Cup-and-ring Marked Rocks and Standing Stones**. Go on a little over a mile and look for a minor road to the right signposted to Mochrum. In Mochrum turn right to find **Druchtag Motte** at the end of the village. Return through the village and at the end of a row of houses turn right on a minor road signposted Elrig and Lochhead. Stay on this road as it bears round to the right. At a crossroads go straight on, signposted Kirkcowan via Drumwalt. At the next T junction turn left, signposted Glenluce.

In less than a mile turn right at the signpost marked Kirkcowan via Drumwalt. You pass **Mochrum Loch** and on the right among trees **Old Place of Mochrum** (private) and continue along a narrow road with passing places over unfenced moorland. A small road enters from the left and then there is a fork below a small house. Keep to the left fork (ignore signpost to Wigtown). Look out for **belted Galloway cattle** in this area. At a T junction with B733 turn right for Kirkcowan. Keep on B733, signposted Wigtown, through Kirkcowan and past the next road junction. You will find **Torhousekie Stone Circle** on the right. Continue on the same road back to Wigtown.

This drive explores the exciting coastline and the remarkable gardens of the Rhins of Galloway, starting from Stranraer. (65 miles, 105km, without counting the distances between the road and garden car parks)

Leave Stranraer by A75. Within 3 miles a signpost indicates **Castle Kennedy Gardens**. After that, continue on A75 to Dunragit where a yellow signpost points to **Glenwhan Garden** on the left. Continue on A75 to the junction with A715. Turn right here for Portpatrick and Drummore. The A748 enters from the right and then you keep left at a fork, still on A715 for Sandhead and Drummore (also RAF Freugh). You now join A716 still going in the same direction. At **Sandhead** take the left fork to go through the village and past the sandy bay. Going in the same direction you rejoin A715 and continue. **Kirkmadrine Church** is signposted to your right. A716 runs by the coast to Ardwell where **Ardwell Gardens** are on your right. Continue on A716 past a large picnic site.

Disregard the turn to Logan Botanic Garden (it will be on your return route) and continue to Drummore, passing a picnic site at **New England Bay**. In Drummore you reach a T junction. Turn right signposted Mull of Galloway. Within a few yards is a signpost Mull of Galloway B7041 to the left. Continue following the signs to **Mull of Galloway**. This is 5 miles, the final 3 over a narrow road with passing places, the last part over a cattle grid and on an unfenced but well surfaced track.

Return by the track and same road to a junction with B7065. Do not bear right for Drummore but go straight on, B7065 for **Port Logan**. At the far end of the sandy bay from the village is the **Fish Pond**. Continue along the coast on B7065 and then inland past two huge farm towers. **Logan Botanic Garden** is on your left. Then continue to the junction with A716, signposted Stranraer. You have to return past Ardwell. Do not go into Sandhead village but keep on A716 and take the left turn B7042 to Portpatrick. Within a mile, near a large farm, is a small signpost marked Portpatrick B7042, and you turn left here. Go past huge farms to a T junction with A77 and turn left for **Portpatrick**, where there is plenty to see. Leave by the way you came but soon turn left on A764 for Leswalt. To the left is a narrow road to **Killantringan Lighthouse**. Keep on A764. Now huge rhododendrons line the road. At a T junction turn right for Leswalt, past a lake and the entrance to **Lochnaw Castle** (now a hotel). In Leswalt turn right on A718, alongside Loch Ryan and back to Stranraer.

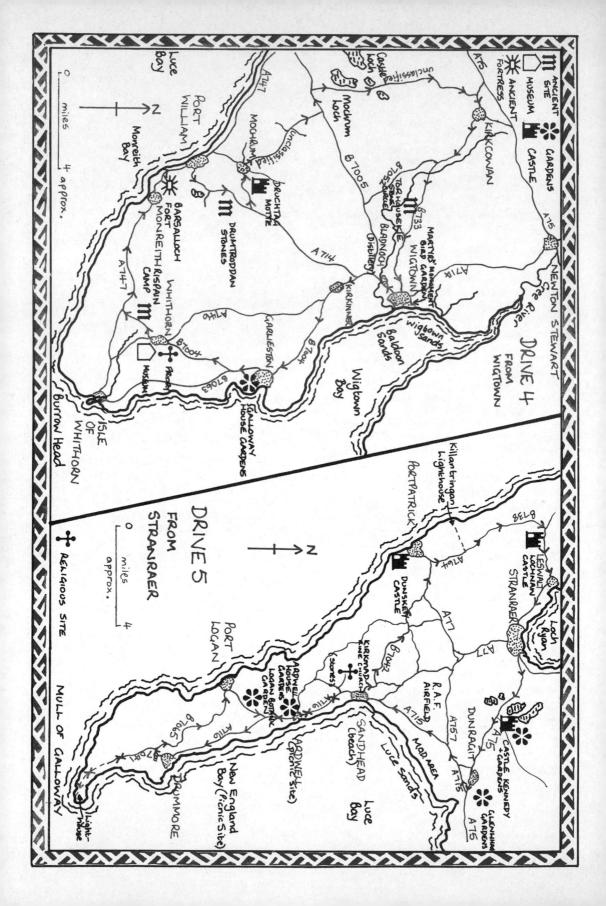

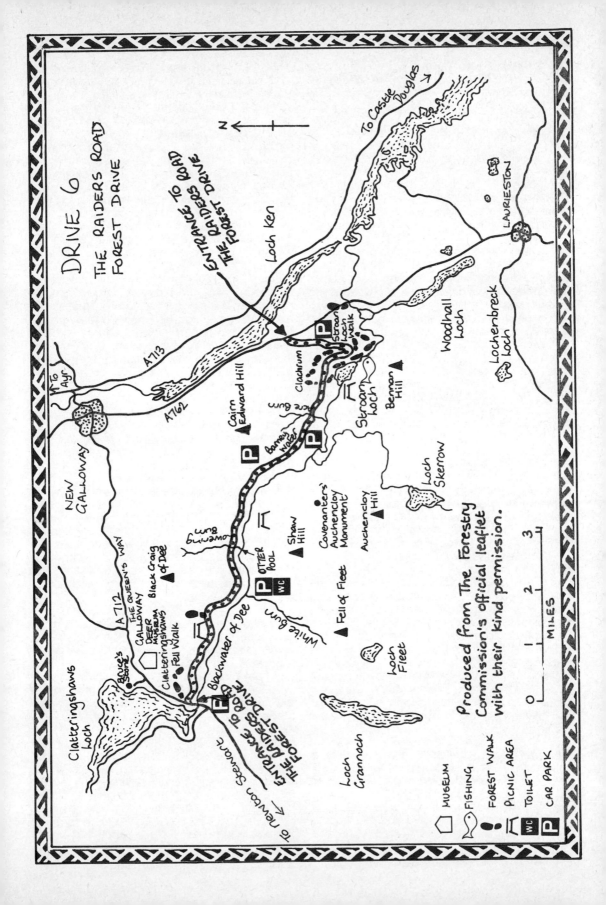

DRIVE 6
THE RAIDERS ROAD
FOREST DRIVE

ENTRANCE TO ROAD
THE RAIDERS FOREST DRIVE

N

To Castle Douglas

Loch Ken

LAURIESTON

A713
To Ayr

A762

NEW GALLOWAY

A712

THE QUEEN'S WAY

Bruce's Stone

GALLOWAY DEER MUSEUM
Fell Walk
Clatteringshaws

Black Craig of Dee

Clatteringshaws Loch

To Newton Stewart

ENTRANCE TO THE RAIDERS FOREST DRIVE

Blackwater of Dee

White Burn

OTTER POOL

Fell of Fleet

Shaw Hill

Burn Laws

Fell of Fleet

Loch Fleet

Loch Grannoch

Covenanters' Auchencloy Monument

Auchencloy Hill

Loch Skerrow

Bennan Hill

Stroan Loch

Loch

Clachrum

Stroan Loch Walk

Cairn Edward Hill

Barney Water

Burn

Woodhall Loch

Lochenbreck Loch

Produced from The Forestry Commission's official leaflet with their kind permission.

MILES
0   1   2   3

MUSEUM

FISHING

FOREST WALK

PICNIC AREA

WC TOILET

P CAR PARK

The ten-mile Raiders' Road Forest Drive runs alongside the River Dee, from Clatteringshaws Loch to Stroan Loch, and you pay £1.00 to enter the road at either end.

Clatteringshaws and Bennan form part of the Galloway Forest Park, which extends to about 240 square miles of forest and moorlands, mountains and lochs. This forest drive is used as a normal timber haulage route in winter, but in summer is opened to visitors, who are requested to drive slowly and take care not to cause any fire hazard or to leave any litter.

The route has an ancient history, having originally been a drove road; and the land it passes through has yielded traces of prehistoric man in the shape of flint spears and arrows and eventually, very late in the day, iron axeheads. In those days, the forest would have been made up of oak and birch thickets, with swampy areas of alder and willow near water. The hunters came in pursuit of deer and wild boar, and possibly even beaver, as well as fish. With plentiful supplies of all of these, there would have been little inducement to settle, clear land and cultivate crops, so there is little evidence of human habitation, though at Crannoch Island near the Otter Pool there do appear to be traces of a 'crannog' or Iron Age round house. Indeed the area was probably still thickly forested in the C14th, at a time when the campaign of Robert the Bruce was fought over this area. On gaining victory in 1314, Bruce rewarded his brother Edward with the Lordship of Galloway, and the hill which overlooks the drive today has been known as Cairn Edward ever since.

From this point on, however, tree clearance was rapid, as land was turned to grazing and wood was used for building and for burning in now established settlements. The fact that the last wolf in Galloway was killed in the 1630s indicates how thin the tree cover had by then become. Evidence of later turbulent times is found in a memorial and martyr's grave not far west of the Black Water, to one of the many Covenanters who were ruthlessly hunted down and slain for their Presbyterian faith in the 1680s.

The character of the area at a later date is romantically evoked in the novel 'The Raiders' by Samuel Rutherford Crockett, which is set at the time of the Jacobite Rising of 1715. Crockett was born not far away, at Little Duchrae, Balmaghie, in 1859 and this was his most popular and successful book, telling the story of gipsy reivers - the Faas and the Marshalls - who steal a herd of cattle from the Maxwells and manage to stampede them across the Brig of the Black Water and into outlaw country. The way in which they do this, setting fire to a mixture of tar and oil on the backs of the unfortunate beasts to make them run, gives the book a dramatic climax. Crockett knew his setting well and portrays it thus: 'A man might ride a long day among the hills of heather and see not one reeking house or any place where kindly folk dwelt. There was a district of thirty miles square in Carrick, in Galloway, and the moors of the Shire over whose border never exciseman put his nose, except with a force of red soldiers at his tail, which did not happen once in twenty years'.

Fierce resistance against the Acts of Enclosure was probably put up here as elsewhere but proved unavailing, and by the mid-C18th the land had changed to a farming scene, supporting hill cattle and large flocks of blackfaced sheep. The viaduct at the Stroan Loch end of the drive remains to remind us of the Victorian age but has not carried trains since 1965.

Over the last 35 years much of the forest has been re-planted, though there are some older plantations near Stroan Loch which are now reaching maturity. The impoversihed soils of the area have difficulty supporting broadleaved trees, though these are planted where possible to give a more varied habitat for wildlife and to enhance the landscape. More successful is the Sitka Spruce, which thrives in Galloway's climate and soil, and is quick to produce timber. Smaller trees are pulped for chipboard and paper-making, while larger ones are used for building timber. You will see examples of typical forest products along the roadside.

The main joy of this drive, however, is in the fact that it runs alongside the River Dee, whose landscapes are the very essence of Galloway, peaceful and unspoilt. Picnic spots are found at each end of the drive, though probably the most picturesque is the one at the Otter Pool. There are regular stopping places for cars and several short walks are clearly indicated, taking visitors through the parts of the forest where they are most likely to see something of the region's rich and varied wildlife, which includes red and roe deer, buzzards, sparrowhawks and ravens, interesting wetland plants and birds at Stroan Loch and - if you are very lucky - otters.

Acknowledgments to the Forestry Commission for material from their Trails leaflets.

The Loch Trool Forest Trail is a circular route round the loch and can be followed in either direction. The most usual starting point is the Caldons Campsite, from which one pursues the Trail in an anti-clockwise direction, but the Bruce's Stone provides a good alternative starting point for those wishing to walk clockwise. There are car parks at both places.

The complete circuit is 4 1/2 miles and takes 3-4 hours but can be shortened if you can arrange to be met with a car along the section between the Bruce's Stone and Glentrool Lodge, which uses the public road. The walk is rough and can be muddy in wet weather, so strong, non-slip footwear is essential.

Starting from the Caldons campsite, follow a road east which leads to a well-marked trail entering a larch plantation. Gaps in the forest here have been caused by storms pulling up trees which were poorly rooted in the thin soil. Presently, you enter a mature Scots pine plantation, where the warm reddish-brown tinge of the bark and the bushy foliage carried high on the trees are characteristic. Among the pines are some magnificent Silver fir and European larch, planted in the late C19th and giving the forest a grandly spacious aspect.

Next you come to a denser, younger plantation, containing a mixture of Japanese larch, Sitka spruce and Scots Pine. The Sitka spruce is readily identifiable by the bluish tinge of its needles. Climbing all the time, you gradually cross the steep, rocky slopes of Mulldonoch and eventually gain fine views over Loch Trool and to the northern hills beyond. Benyellary stands above the valley of the Buchan Burn, and Buchan House sits under Buchan Hill to your right, while to the left you see the precipitous, heather-clad Fell of Eschoncan.

Bennan and Benyellary are both clothed up to the planting limit of 450 metres (1475 feet) with Sitka spruce, Japanese larch and Lodgepole pine. Experience has proved that planting at 600 metres, which has been attempted successfully in other parts of the country, is not successful in Galloway. One of the best views of the Merrick, which at 844 metres (2770 feet) is the highest hill in the Southern Uplands, is gained from the viewpoint at the Torr, just off this section of the Trail. This stretch is also reputed to have been where King Robert the Bruce of Scotland ambushed an English force in 1307, bombarding them with an avalanche of boulders and then pursuing any survivors to the Steps of Trool and completing the butchery there.

The trail's eastern extremity is marked by the footbridge over the Glenhead Burn, and at this point it bids farewell to the Southern Upland Way, the coast-to-coast route with which it has shared the route since Caldons Wood. Anyone you meet who is doing the Southern Upland Way has undertaken a walk of 212 miles in all!

The Trail now follows the Gairland Burn, which is at its most spectacular after rain or, more appropriately, after melting snow - appropriately because it was melting glaciers after the last Ice Age which scoured out this very landscape. Mounds of rubble and boulders, now overgrown, can still be identified as the debris from this great movement of ice and meltwaters.

At Glenhead and Buchan you will find the last remnants of the ancient natural oak forest, similar to the oakwood at Caldons. These are sessile oaks, with distinctively stalked leaves, sharing the woods with a certain amount of alder, birch and hazel. Until the end of the last century, the oaks were regularly coppiced to provide a fast growing supply of oak bark for the tanning industry and wood for the charcoal makers. Looking at the trees, you will easily be able to see the evidence of coppicing in the past, which leaves a stump or 'stool' from which numerous small shoots rapidly grow. Today, although coppicing is no longer carried out, the woods are managed in such a way as to preserve them, as they are, in fact, protected as a Site of Special Scientific Interest.

You come next to the stretch of road already mentioned, between the Gairland Burn and the Bruce's Stone around Buchan House. Standing on the Earl of Galloway's Bridge, you will be able to see the Buchan Falls. The Bruce's Stone commemorates that same battle in 1307, which proved to be a turning point in the fortunes of the Scots and culminated in their victory at Bannockburn seven years later, in 1314.

Passing the private grounds of Glentrool Lodge, the Trail leaves the public road and crosses Kenmure Moss, where the plantations are of Norway spruce at the north end, Sitka spruce and Lodgepole pine in the boggy middle part, and Japanese larch on the drier, higher ground to the south. Again, fine views are enjoyed to the hills of Mulldonoch, Lamachan, Cambrick and Craignaw. A short loch-side section returns to the Caldons campsite.

Acknowledgments to The Forestry Commission for material from their Trails leaflets.

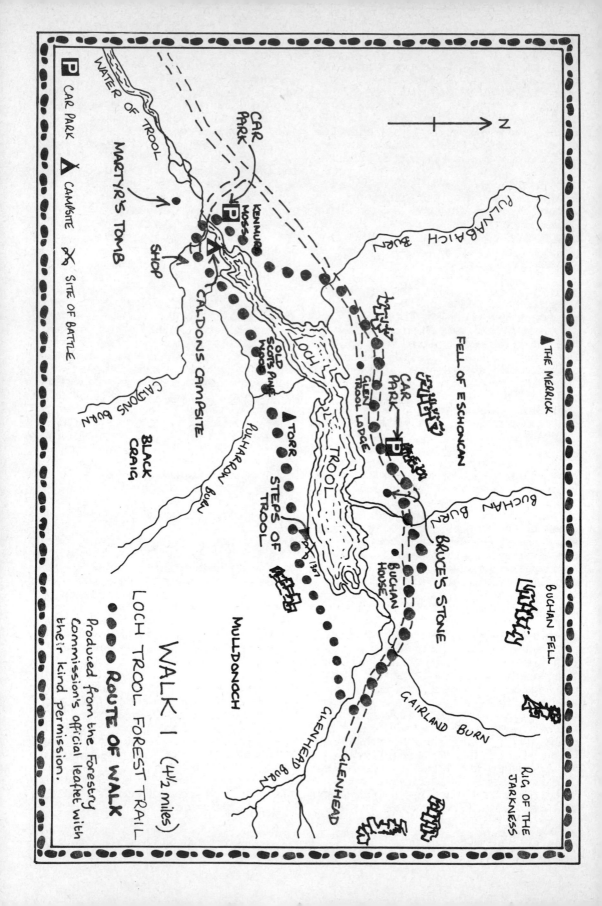

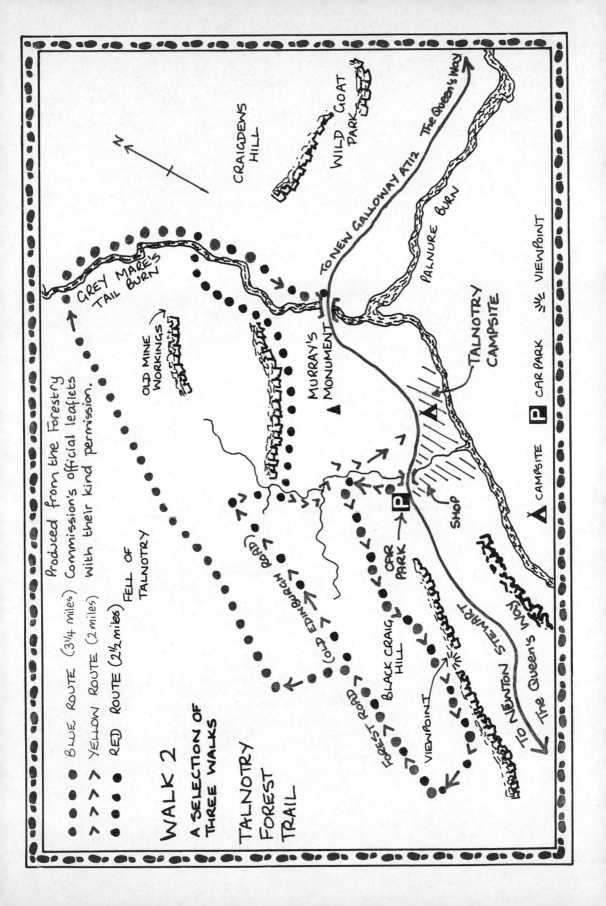

The Talnotry Forest Trail actually offers three trails to follow: the Blue Route, which takes about 21/2 hours and traces an irregular-shaped path around Murray's Monument; and the red and yellow routes, both of which stay within the area circumscribed by the Blue Route and use parts of it, but take respectively about 2 hours and 1 1/2 hours.

All the trails have some steep sections, it is important to wear suitable, non-slip footwear. Please also be sure to follow the country code and guard against risk of fire, leave no litter, fasten any gates, control dogs and take care not to damage any wildlife, plants or trees.

All three trails start together from the A712 (the Queen's Way) opposite the entrance to the Talnotry Campsite. They head up a burn into the forest and then go left up a ride across the face of Black Craig. The trees here are mainly Japanese larch, which is deciduous, losing its needles in autumn after turning a rich golden colour and growing them again as bright tufts of green in the spring; and Scots and Lodgepole pines, which grow their needles in pairs, the Scots pine being dark, bluish green, and the Lodgepole pine being a bright or deep green.

After a slight dip, the joint trails come out of the trees to give splendid views over what was once a glacial valley. The Palnure Burn and the Queen's Way wind along the valley floor, overhung by rugged and forested slopes, whose most dramatic feature is the huge granite hill at Craignelder, known as Cairnsmore of Fleet.

Despite the smooth outlines of this range, the slopes glint with naked rock of igneous origin and are very rough, scoured out by the glaciers which once forged their passage down this valley towards Wigtown Bay, which is visible in the distance. On a clear day, indeed, you can see much further, to the Mull of Galloway and even to the Isle of Man.

Skirting an outcrop, the trails then drop steeply to join a forest road on the line of the Old Edinburgh Road, which was once a pilgrim route to Whithorn and a highway to Ireland. Turning right along the road, you will note that the trees are now mainly Lodgepole Pine and Sitka spruce, the pines with their bushy crowns and the spruces with their more erect leading shoots. Sitka spruce have very sharp needles, characteristically silver blue on the undersides.

It is at this point that the routes separate. The Blue Route veers to the right and climbs gradually to the summit of the trail at 230 metres. So severe are the winds up here that the trees have difficulty in surviving, but the views are magnificent, looking along the Palnure Valley towards the sea, and also inland, past Craigdews Hill to Clatteringshaws Loch. A long traverse across the hillside takes the walker down towards Murray's Monument, commemorating Alexander Murray, born the son of a local shepherd in 1775, who later became Professor of Oriental Languages at Edinburgh University.

The Grey Mare's Tail Burn is crossed at a bridge and followed downstream by means of a steep section where care must be taken to stay back from the gorge and stick to the forest side of the fence. If you are fortunate enough to be visiting after a period of rain, you will see the water of the burn tumbling and cascading down a series of spectacular waterfalls. The trail and burn both level out as they meet the Old Edinburgh Road again.

The Red and Yellow Trails, meanwhile, have continued along the forest road. Markers indicate the point at which, after following the route down through the trees alongside a small burn, the Yellow Trail turns for home, while the Red Trail takes a different upward route, giving a great view of the road and waterfalls which are now deep down below. Turning upstream, the Red Trail follows the lip of the gorge and eventually returns to the forest road after passing a now flooded (and sealed off) former lead-mine. There were once numerous mine workings in the area but many of the spoil heaps are now concealed by vegetation.

The forest road crosses the Grey Mare's Tail Burn by a bridge and at this point the Red Trail is rejoined by the Blue one, and the two Trails continue the descent along the burn, past another series of impressive waterfalls.

The road is regained at the Goat Park under Craigdews Hill. Several areas of Galloway still have herds of feral goats, which can do untold damage to young trees, so they have to be excluded from tree plantations. Here, they have been captured and released within an enclosure, where they can be easily seen by the public without being a nuisance to the forester.

Murray's Monument stands nearby and those visitors energetic enough to manage another climb to the obelisk will be rewarded with a fine view.

Acknowledgments to the Forestry Commission for material from their Trails leaflets.

The Kirroughtree Forest Trails are to be found at the southern end of the Galloway Forest Park, and run through the oldest Forestry Commission plantations in the south of Scotland.

Kirroughtree used to be the heart of the whole Forestry Commission operation, with its own tree nursery producing trees from seed gathered on the west coast of America. At the peak period, up to the late 1970s, some one million seedling and transplant trees were produced here annually and these trees then furnished the forests of Scotland and the north of England.

Sitka spruce was the most commonly planted tree and some of these plantations, now at full maturity after some fifty years, are in the process of being thinned. The soft timber is then processed for chipboard, paper, pallets, fencing and pulp, while larger trees are cut into timber for building use.

In upland areas, however, thinning is not viable as strong winds will then blow down the remaining large trees, so clear-felling and replanting is the only alternative. After lying fallow for a year, the land is ready to support a new crop of trees and the forester then has the opportunity to plant a new landscape.

These days, the much-criticised square block layouts of former years have been abandoned and the forester plants to follow the natural contours of the land, being careful to enhance any natural features such as streams and to create as balanced and varied a habitat as possible for wildlife. While spruce, therefore, is still the most commonly planted tree, considerable areas are now given over to broadleaved trees, such as beech, birch, oak and rowan. The progress of a new forest of this sort is remarkably rapid and regular visitors will know how completely the appearance of the landscape can change in only a few years.

The Kirroughtree Trails offer a variety of different walks, which visitors can select according to their personal taste. The Trails leave the forest road in places and stout footwear is therfore essential. As in all forests, please be especially careful not to cuase any risk of fire, not to damage the plants or wildlife, and not to leave any litter.

Three of the four Trails start by walking through mature plantations to the top of Blackcraig Hill, and along the way you will pass spoil heaps from some of the old lead workings which used to network this area from the early C18th onwards. You may see the glint of lead ore, a reminder that silver was also extracted here, for most lead contains a small percentage of the more precious metal. Since their closure in the early years of this century, most of the mines have been capped, though you will still see the entries to some of the 'adits' or horizontal mine shafts. Where you see 'lade' marked on the Trail, this indicates the channel which brought water from the Bruntis Loch to be used for sifting the silver from the lead.

The longest of the Trails is the Larg Hill Trail, which is a four-mile route and takes about 2 1/2 hours to walk. It is marked by blue posts and goes through an area which has been felled and recently re-stocked. If you choose to enter this trail from the northern end, via the car park on the Queen's Way, you will add a mile to the overall distance. Either way, you will be afforded magnificent views over Newton Stewart and across to the east over the hills of Cairnsmore of Fleet.

The Viewpoint Trail, with red marker posts, is 2 1/2 miles long and takes about 1 1/2 hours to walk, again giving fine views over Cairnsmore of Fleet, but also offering a marvellous panorama south over the River Cree estuary. On a clear day you may be able to see as far as the Isle of Man.

The Bruntis Trail is the shortest, at 1 1/2 miles and takes about an hour to walk. It shares part of the route of the longer Trails but diverts to the Bruntis Lochs at the top of Blackcraig Hill. Both lochs were formed by damming the river to give a water supply for the lead mines - but today they are mainly used by fishermen and the larger is regularly stocked with rainbow trout.

Finally, the Bluebell Trail adopts a completely different route and is marked by white posts. It is a 2 mile route and can be completed in little over an hour, though you may wish to spend longer enjoying the Forest Garden. The walk is aptly named, for in spring the woods here are a sea of bluebells. The Trail is enjoyable in summer and autumn too, however, for in summer the young leaves of the beech trees throw a pretty dappled shade, while in the autumn the larches turn colour and shed their needles to carpet the ground in gold. There are several paths through the Forest Garden and a leaflet is available that will identify the tree species within it.

Acknowledgments to The Forestry Commission for material from their Trails leaflets.

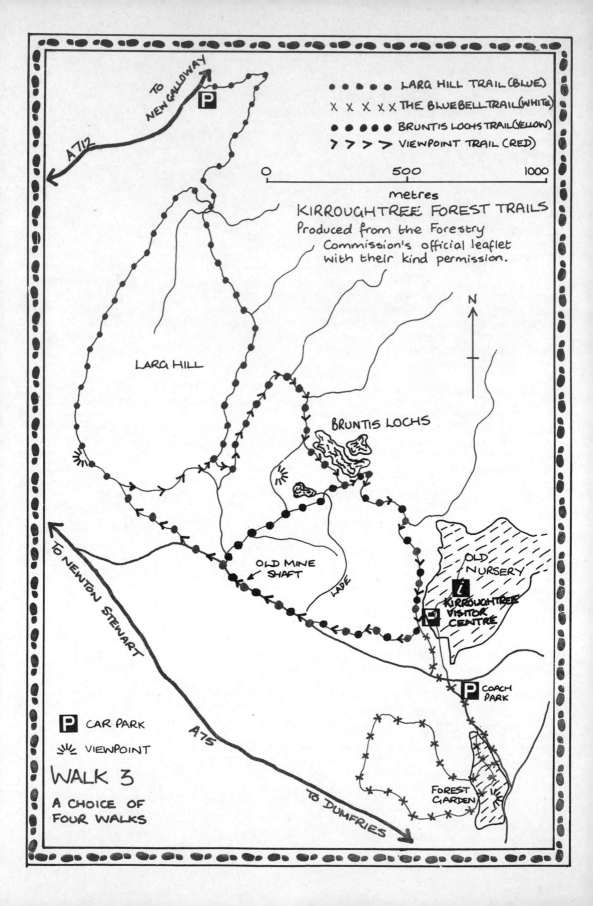

TO NEW GALLOWAY

A712

• • • • • LARG HILL TRAIL (BLUE)
X X X X X X THE BLUEBELL TRAIL (WHITE)
● ● ● ● ● BRUNTIS LOCHS TRAIL (YELLOW)
〉 〉 〉 〉 〉 VIEWPOINT TRAIL (RED)

0   500   1000
metres

KIRROUGHTREE FOREST TRAILS
Produced from the Forestry
Commission's official leaflet
with their kind permission.

N

LARG HILL

BRUNTIS LOCHS

TO NEWTON STEWART

OLD MINE SHAFT

LADE

OLD NURSERY

KIRROUGHTREE VISITOR CENTRE

COACH PARK

P CAR PARK
☀ VIEWPOINT

WALK 3

A CHOICE OF FOUR WALKS

A75

TO DUMFRIES

FOREST GARDEN

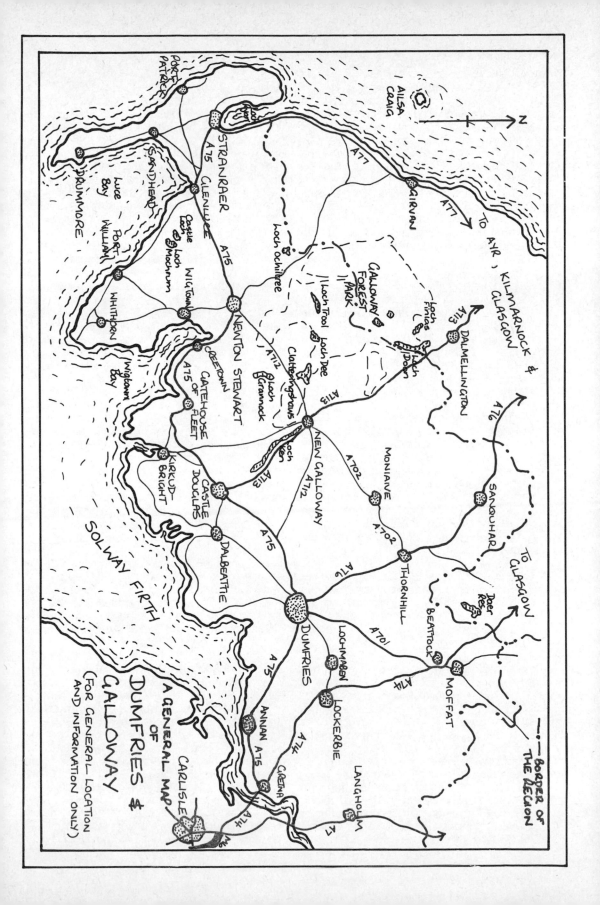

The Southern Upland Way

When in the year 1618 John Taylor set out from London to undertake a walking tour of Scotland, he did so partly to settle a bet, but also to be 'an eye-witness of divers things which I had heard of that country'. And walking, many would still say, is the best way to get to know a country. John Taylor's first day on Scottish soil saw him cover the 40 miles from Carlisle to Moffat, during which journey he was obliged to wade across both the River Esk and the River Annan. Long-distance walkers today are not required to undertake such a baptism - indeed, on the whole their needs are well catered for.

In particular, Dumfries and Galloway is fortunate in being crossed by the Southern Upland Way, one of only three long-distance footpaths so far created in Scotland. The western half of this coast-to-coast route runs through the heart of the region, from Portpatrick on the Mull of Galloway in the west to Beattock, near Moffat, in the east, through all its varied scenery, before crossing into the neighbouring Borders region.

Though there are some shorter sections which are suitable for family groups or less experienced walkers, many of the upland sections are very long and arduous and should only be attempted by those who are both fit and properly equipped. Although the path is waymarked, the route is not always easy to follow - especially in poor weather - and anyone setting out on the upland sections should be prepared to make use of map and compass if necessary.

The Southern Upland Way may be joined at any convenient point, and excursions planned to suit both the ability of the group and the weather. Remember that the weather can change quickly in this part of the world - so be prepared for the worst.

Anyone planning to tackle all, or even part of the route through Dumfries and Galloway is strongly advised to invest in a copy of the Official Guide and Route Map for the Southern Upland Way (Western Section) available from H.M.S.O. and bookshops. The map covers the whole of the route within the region, and the 'Way' is clearly marked. In addition, the Guide describes features of interest along the route and has excellent advice on preparation and safety. A separate leaflet is published, giving up-to-date information on accommodation and services along the 'Way'. This is available from local tourist offices and from the Countryside Commission for Scotland, Battleby, Redgorton, Perth, PH1 3EW.

Two sections of the Way in Dumfries and Galloway are considered suitable for less experienced walkers. The first is the 37km (23 miles) between Portpatrick and Glenluce. This first section of the Way follows the coast for some distance past the rugged cliff scenery and Killantringan lighthouse, before striking inland through rolling farmland across the Rhinns towards Stranraer, most of it being easy walking along lanes or tracks. Skirting the town, it then passes through Castle Kennedy, with its beautiful grounds and gardens, before making its way into the hill and forest country beyond and through the conifers of Glenwhan. Once the route crosses the unclassified road south of New Luce, the walking becomes more difficult, as it reaches the desolate moorland.

A second short section of about 12 km (7miles) between Bargrennan on the A714 and the head of Loch Trool, all of it through the Glentrool Forest, also provides some relatively easy walking, with beautiful views.

Other sections of the Southern Upland Way take you through a variety of terrain, from the undulating country between New Luce and Bargrennan to the more dramatic hill country of the Galloway Forest beyond Glentrool; from the grouse moors of the Western Lowther Hills to the great route-way of Annandale. No brief account such as this can hope to give a real idea of the Way, nor of the interesting country it passes through, nor of the exhilaration of the long upland stretches. Inaugurated only in 1984, the route is already popular.

Those planning to walk the route without the support of a vehicle will do well to plan their route well in advance, and to check on the availability of accommodation. Advance booking is necessary, especially during the high summer season and in the low season, or at popular holiday times. A number of camping sites, and a limited amount of 'bothy' accommodation are also available along the Way. Details are included in the information leaflet. Also in the leaflet are details of organisations offering guided walks and treks. Users of the Way may meet Countryside Rangers, staff specially employed by the Regional Council to patrol and maintain the footpath, and to provide advice and information for walkers.

Let us hope that, at the end of a good day's walking, we may be able to echo John Taylor's words describing his arrival in Moffat in 1618, 'At night being come to the towne, I found good ordinary countrey entertainment; my fare and my lodging were sweet and good'.

Until the union of Scotland and England, conflict had been endemic and fortificiation a necessity. Grand families lived in stone castles, the lesser lairds in defensive tower houses. When times became peaceful, comfort and convenience became more important and many tower houses were left to fall into ruin, while others were incorporated into more comfortable residences. LOCHNAW CASTLE, now a hotel, is an example of such rebuilding. The home of the Agnews, it was originally an early C16th oblong tower, to which adjacent ranges were added in 1663. It was further enlarged in the C19th, though much of this later addition has since been removed. MAXWELTON HOUSE also incorporates an earlier tower.

That conflict was no longer a threat is clear from DRUMLANRIG, completed in 1690, with a great sweeping entrance stair, undoubtedly a castle but in no way a fortress like Caerlaverock. By the mid-C18th the classical style was in fashion. MOFFAT HOUSE, now a hotel, was designed by John Adam of the famous Adam family for the Earl of Hopetoun, a plain and dignified three-storey central block with two lower symmetrical wings and characteristic tall C18th windows. Another notable classical house, built about 1760 for Alexander Murray by Robert Mylne, was CALLY HOUSE, now the Cally Palace Hotel, though without the pillared portico which was added in 1833. Now with later additions, the nucleus of GALLOWAY HOUSE has the typical plan of a central main block linked to two frontal pavilions, and here the classical style is further emphasised by the pediment over the entrance. At ARBIGLAND HOUSE (very occasionally open to the public) classical taste is further illustrated by the addition of urns to the roof-line. The extensive and beautiful grounds of both these latter houses are open to the public. See 'Gardens of the Area'.

During the C19th, greatly influenced by Sir Walter Scott, people began to take pride in their Scottish origins and to look to the past of their own country rather than to that of Greece and Rome. Stonework, turrets and towers reminiscent of old fortified castles became fashionable, a style, further encouraged by the royal family's purchase and re-building of Balmoral,which has since become known as 'Scottish Baronial'. Visitors to Castle Kennedy gardens will see the grandiose LOCHINCH CASTLE (not open to the public) with its gables, turrets and parapets, built in 1864-67 for the Earl of Stair, while those visiting Threave Gardens will catch sight of the castellated THREAVE HOUSE. CRAIGCLEUGH HOUSE,

now the Scottish Explorers' Museum, is an imposing mansion with its tower, mullioned windows and tall chimneys reminiscent of Jacobean architecture, and another museum, SHAMBELLIE HOUSE, is a scaled-down version of Scottish Baronial taste, suitable for a country gentleman. This style spread also to hotels, of which that at Portpatrick is a fine example.

DRUMLANRIG CASTLE North of Thornhill, and signposted on all major routes. A grand mansion in pink sandstone built between 1679 and 1690, probably incorporating parts of an older Douglas Castle. It is built round an open courtyard with a circular staircase tower in each inner corner and four great square towers to the outside, each surmounted by four turrets. A cross between a castle and a palace, Drumlanrig has long been admired as one of the first and most important Renaissance houses in Scotland. 'Drumlanrig,' said Defoe in 1724, 'is like a fine picture in a dirty grotto ... 'tis environed with mountains and that of the wildest and most hideous aspect', going on to wonder at 'a palace so glorious, gardens so fine and everything so truly magnificent' in such a place. William Douglas, Duke of Queensberry, who built it, spent only one night in it, so horrified was he by the final cost. Drumlanrig had been handed down from father to son through thirteen generations of Douglases until 1810, when the line died out and it passed into the possession of Henry Scott, who became Duke of Buccleuch as well as Duke of Queensberry. The service wings on either side of the forecourt were added in the C19th. The house is lavishly decorated and full of treasures, fine furniture, great paintings and beautiful ceramics. Formal gardens surround it and with its romantic appearance, pink sandstone and turrets, it is a favourite with many people. Today they can also enjoy an adventure playground, nature trail, tea room and gift shop, as well as a working craft centre. The grounds are open all season but the house only until mid-August. Closed in winter.

MAXWELTON HOUSE East of Moniaive, off B729. A C17th house incorporating the round tower of the old Glencairn Castle, which was later modernised and then completely restored in the 1960s with appropriate antique furniture and fittings. Famous as the home of Annie Laurie of the famous love-song, courted by William Douglas in the C18th, though they never, in the end, married. With a chapel and small museum of farm and domestic implements. Gardens open a limited amount all season, house only in July and August. Check opening times. Closed in winter.

The easiest form of castle to construct was a motte, a large earth mound which could be thrown up comparatively quickly, requiring little more than plenty of labour, and then surmounted by wooden defences. Large stone castles needing expert builders were costly and slow to achieve and were constructed only by kings or noble families, to be at once fortification, prestige residence and symbol of power. Conflict was a way of life, and in the C15th and C16th large numbers of rectangular stone tower houses were built, to serve the local lairds as homes which could be defended and as bases for raiding or cattle thieving. The following list does not include all tower houses in private ownership.

CAERLAVEROCK CASTLE South-east of Dumfries, signposted from B725. Situated in low-lying ground without natural defences, this castle is surrounded by a moat and earth rampart. Its shape is unique in Britain, a triangle with round towers at two corners and, at the third, double towers with a gate beneath, solidly built in red sandstone. Dating from the end of the C13th, neither the original builder nor owner is known but it was beseiged and taken by Edward I in 1300. Over the next three centuries, as the fortunes of war changed, the castle at times suffered 'destructions' from both English and Scots. By the C15th it was in the hands of the Maxwells, who improved the defences and whose crest is carved above the gateway. After the union of the two kingdoms it was made more comfortable as a dwelling by the addition in 1634 of the Renaissance mansion with spacious staircase, large windows, fireplaces and latrines. But in 1640, defended for Charles I by Robert Maxwell, it gave in after a 13 week seige and bombardment by the Covenanters. Thereafter it was partly destroyed, to prevent further trouble.

CARDONESS CASTLE South-west of Gatehouse-of- Fleet, signposted on A75. C15th tower house overlooking the Water of Fleet. This tower with its forbidding exterior is an excellent example of a C15th laird's dwelling. By their standards it was comfortable, with service and storage rooms on the ground floor, a grand hall occupying the first, and above that two bedchambers and then an attic. The main rooms all had fireplaces and good-sized windows with stone bench seats, and there was a latrine on each floor.

CARSLUITH CASTLE West of Gatehouse- of- Fleet, signposted on A75. A C16th tower house with the armorial of the Brown family. A later wing and stair turret were added to the original tower which had a conventional layout of service rooms at ground level, hall on the first floor and bedchambers and attic above.

CASTLE KENNEDY East of Stranraer, signposted from A75. Early C17th house, sadly destroyed by fire in 1716, a five-storey block with towers either side and two-storey ranges added later, once a comfortable and well furnished home. Beautiful gardens now surround the ruin.

CASTLE OF PARK West of Glenluce, off the A75. May be viewed from the outside only. Built by Thomas Hay of Park in 1590, this imposing tower house stands high above the water of Luce. With its four storeys, garret and steep roof it is typical of a Galloway laird's home.

COMLONGON CASTLE South-east of Dumfries, on B724. A well preserved C15th tower house of stout red sandstone. The walls are very thick, the north wall being 4.1m in depth with small vaulted chambers built into it. The hall on the first floor is unusual in having two fireplaces, one grand with pillars on either side and a carved cornice, the other for a kitchen which could be screened off. The chambers on the 2nd and 3rd floors have fireplaces, windows with bench seats, and latrines. Adjoining the tower is a mansion built in the C19th, now a hotel.

CRAIGCAFFIE CASTLE North-east of Stranraer. Off A77 on minor road. Visible from outside only. Small C16th tower house.

DRUCHTAG MOTTE North-east of Port William, just north of Mochrum village. An excellent example of a C12th motte, with mound, deep ditch and counterscarp bank, exactly as the Normans are shown building in the Bayeux Tapestry, though lacking the wooden defences.

DRUMCOLTRAN CASTLE South-west of Dumfries, near Kirkgunzeon, off A711. A plain and severe tower, with the windows enlarged and the interior re-arranged and sub-divided in the C18th, standing proudly over farm buildings which now cluster round it.

DRUMLANRIG CASTLE See 'Historic Houses'.

DUNSKEY CASTLE Portpatrick. Spectacular cliff-top setting. Possibly on the site of an earlier castle, the tower was built by William Adair of Kinhult early in the C16th. The original block was L shaped with the public rooms on the first floor and private chambers above also two dark prison cells at ground level.

GILNOCKIE TOWER South of Langholm. Clearly visible from A7 but can only be viewed from outside. C16th tower house with walls 2m thick, once the home of the notorious Border reiver Johnnie Armstrong.

HODDOM CASTLE South-west of Ecclefechan, off B725. Massive C16th tower house built by John Maxwell, Lord Herries, as his chief stronghold. A beacon platform built out from the north gate enabled the watch to light a signal whenever an English incursion threatened. A further watch tower, known as Repentance, possibly because it was built from the ruins of a former chapel, stands to the south. The castle grounds are now a caravan park.

LOCH DOON CASTLE By Loch Doon, signposted from A713. The substantial remains of an early C14th castle, with walls almost 2m thick and still standing some 8m high. The eleven-sided curtain wall was built to fit an island in the lake. When the hydro-electric scheme meant raising the water level, the castle was dismantled stone by stone and re-erected on its present site on the shore.

LOCHMABEN CASTLE West of Lockerbie, signposted from B7020 and A709. The much reduced ruins of a castle first built in the C13th and added to over the years. Originally in Bruce hands, it was of vital strategic importance, taken by Edward I, recaptured by the Douglases and later a residence of King James IV, when a great hall was built. James V was at Lochmaben when the Scots army was defeated at the disastrous battle of Solway Moss.

LOCHNAW CASTLE See 'Historic Houses'.

MACLELLAN'S CASTLE Kirkcudbright, in the town centre. Large C16th tower house built by Sir Thomas MacLellan, provost of Kirkcudbright, and in spite of its apparent fortifications essentially a domestic house, with large windows, heated rooms, stairs and closets, but still traditional in being centred round a first floor hall with an imposing fireplace.

MORTON CASTLE North of Thornhill, by Morton Loch, near minor road from A702. Not open to the public but visible from the outside. C14th Douglas castle. Situated with no defensive advantages and with a grand hall with large windows, this may have been a country dwelling or hunting lodge.

MOTTE OF URR North of Dalbeattie, off B794. The earthworks of a C12th motte and bailey castle, the largest in Scotland, once belonging to a minor branch of the Balliol family. The motte itself, surrounded by its own ditch is set within an elongated bailey defended by a further 15m wide ditch. The huge scale of the work is such that it almost needs to be seen from the air to be properly appreciated.

OLD PLACE OF MOCHRUM West of Wigtown, near Mochrum Loch. Visible from the road. Two early C16th towers joined by a later addition. Not open to the public.

ORCHARDTON TOWER South-east of Castle Douglas, signposted on A711. C15th tower house and the only cylindrical one in Scotland, although they are familiar in Ireland. Originally belonging to the Cairns family it passed to the Maxwells. The thick walls leave small rooms inside but they were built to some degree of comfort.

STRANRAER CASTLE C16th tower house built by the Adairs of Kinhult. Built to the standard three storey plan with the hall on the first floor, it was altered about 1820 when the top storey was added and the first floor converted into a courtroom with prisoners' cells on the second and third. In 1682 the tower was the headquarters from which John Graham of Claverhouse carried out his notorious persecution of the Covenanters.

THREAVE CASTLE West of Castle Douglas, signposted from A75. Car park and then 0.8km walk. A small boat can ferry visitors to the island on which the castle stands. Of particular interest is the small medieval harbour. First built in the C14th, Threave was the stronghold of the Black Douglases. It stands as a huge defensive tower into which entrance was by wooden stair. Directly above was a platform from which missiles could be dropped onto the heads of any attackers. The kitchens, storage, well and dungeons were below. The great hall on the first floor had a fine fireplace and large windows with stone seats. On the second floor were the private chambers, while the quarters for the garrison occupied the third. A spiral stair went up one angle wall, while another provided space for the latrines. The Douglases became too powerful for the king's liking, and the castle had to surrender after a two month siege by King James II, when the great cannon, Mons Meg, was used against it. The king then appointed custodians to hold it, the last being the Maxwells, staunch adherents of the royal family, who resisted the Covenanters on behalf of Charles I until ordered to lay down their arms. The castle was then partly dismantled to prevent any further trouble.

NEOLITHIC & BRONZE AGE MONUMENTS

The region has a large number of cairns and stones from the 2nd and 3rd millenia BC. The neolithic burial cairns are the earliest monuments. The purpose of cup-and-ring markings is obscure, numerous theories from sun-worship to metal prospecting having been put forward. The exact use of stone circles is also unknown. Amongst the many sites the following are particularly famous.

BALCRAIG CUP-AND-RING MARKINGS North-west of Whithorn, off B7021. Under a protective covering in fields normally in cultivation. Rock faces with cup-and-ring markings.

BARGRENNAN CHAMBERED CAIRN West of Glentrool village, in forestry plantation with restricted access. A much reduced cairn but one which has given its name to a type of passage grave.

CAIRNHOLY CHAMBERED CAIRNS South-west of Gatehouse-of-Fleet, signposted from A75. The best long cairns in the area and among the earliest neolithic remains. CAIRNHOLY I was originally a long straight-sided mound which has lost most of its overlying cairn material but which is left with its huge side slabs, probably the nucleus of the tomb, its antechamber and a facade of eight tall stones. CAIRNHOLY II was robbed of much of its original cairn to provide building stone in the C18th but the great slabs of the inner and outer chambers remain, with one large cap-stone, and two tall stones at the entrance.

DRUMTRODDAN CUP-AND-RING MARKINGS South-west of Wigtown, clearly signposted, off A714, reached by a farm track. A railed enclosure in a field with several groups of cup-and-ring markings on exposed stone outcrops.

DRUMTRODDAN STANDING STONES 365m to the south, an alignment of three standing stones, 3m high of which the middle stone has fallen.

HIGH BANKS CUP-AND-RING MARKINGS A minor road southeast from Kirkcudbright and a farm track leading south-east of High Banks farm. A large rock sheet with a remarkable display of cups-and-rings in a variety of patterns. Casts of this prehistoric art can be seen in the Stewartry Museum in Kirkcudbright.

LAGGANGARN STANDING STONES On open moorland near the head of Tarff Water. A pair of standing stones which are a landmark for walkers on the Southern Upland Way but require a long walk over open moorland where it is easy to lose the way. Christian crosses have been inscribed on them but the stones are almost certainly of prehistoric origin.

MID-GLENIRON CHAMBERED CAIRN North of Glenluce Abbey. Much-ruined cairns and long chambered tombs of historical importance but little visual interest.

TORHOUSKIE STONE CIRCLE W of Wigtown, signposted beside B733. One of the best preserved of its kind in Britain, this is a circle of 19 rather dumpy granite boulders, on slightly raised ground. The stones are graded in height and the circle is flattened where the larger stones have been placed. In the centre, a smaller central stone with a great boulder either side, have been set to face the larger stones. A standing stone to the south and an alignment of three stones to the east may have played a significant part in the original design. This circle is similar to some recumbent stone circles in North East Scotland but is unlike others in the Galloway region. What sort of ceremony took place in the circle is unknown.

'TWELVE APOSTLES' HOLYWOOD STONE CIRCLE North of Dumfries, in fields beside a minor road running north-west from New Bridge. Six standing and five fallen stones form the largest stone circle on the mainland of Scotland and the fifth largest in Britain, spread across two fields. The largest stone, now fallen, is 3.2m long and the circle has similarities to circles in Cumbria. At one time there may have been twelve stones but the circle does, of course, pre-date the apostles by some 2000 years.

'THE WREN'S EGG' BLAIRBUIE STANDING STONES South-east of Port William, near a farm track off a minor road between A747 and A714. A large boulder, a glacial erratic, with a pair of standing stones.

IRON AGE & ROMAN REMAINS

Many hill forts and camps can now be recognised only by ditches and mounds which outline their plan.

ARDWELL POINT 'DOON CASTLE' BROCH South of Sandhead. On a rocky promontary by the coast, the remains of a broch (a circular defended dwelling) recognisable though much reduced in height. It had entrances to seaward and to landward, the latter defended by a wall and natural gully.

BARSALLOCH FORT South of Port William, signposted on A747, with steep climb by footpath. An iron-age fortification backing on to a cliff above the sea and defended by a curved ditch and ramparts on the landward side.

BIRRENS ROMAN FORT South-east of Lockerbie. Excavation, research and aerial photography have provided a complete picture of this fort. Finds from the site are displayed in the Dumfries Museum.

BURNSWARK HILL FORT AND ROMAN CAMPS North-east of Ecclefechan. A minor road from B725 runs north to the hill. Around the twin summits are the ramparts of an iron-age fort, large enough to have been a tribal centre. On either side are Roman camps, one with three artillery platforms directed toward the fort. These appear to be ancient siege works, able to throw sling bolts and ballista balls into the fort. But no such siege is recorded and it is now thought that the Romans may have been using an abandoned native fort for military exercises and artillery practice.

CASTLE HAVEN DUN On the shore at Kirkandrews south of Gatehouse-of-Fleet. The only galleried dun (a fortified homestead) in Galloway. Cleared and largely rebuilt in 1905, the dun is D shaped with an entrance from the land and a stepped gateway leading to the shore. The thick walls contain three narrow galleries, with openings to the interior. The outer enclosure may have been added later. The dun seems still to have been in use in medieval times.

CASTLE O'ER FORT South of Eskdalemuir, in a forestry plantation with restricted access. An impressive site with successive phases of construction.

DURISDEER ROMAN FORT Near Durisdeer, Nithsdale. A small fort probably built to assist the main forts in controlling the countryside.

GLENLOCHAR ROMAN FORT Northwest of Castle Douglas. The previous existence of a Roman fort here was revealed by aerial photography.

KEMP'S WALK FORT West of Stranraer, overlooking Broadsea Bay at Labrax. Three lines of ramparts defended the landward approach while steep slopes provided protection on the seaward side.

MOTE OF MARK South of Dalbeattie at Rockcliffe. National Trust for Scotland. Signposted footpath from Rockcliffe. Evidently an important citadel, the summit was defended by a massive rampart of timber and dry-stone construction, now only a low bank. Finds have included jewellery, metal-work, glass inlay and enamel, as well as beads, jet and pottery from overseas, testifying to the princely life-style of the Celtic chieftains. Legends associate the hill with King Mark, Tristan and Iseult, and it was certainly occupied at a time consistent with their story. The great rampart was attacked and burnt in the C7th, with a fire so fierce that the granite stones have vitrified. Later it was occupied simply by squatters.

MULL OF GALLOWAY EARTHWORKS The road to the Mull lighthouse crosses two lines of earthworks but the reason for their construction is a matter for speculation.

RAEBURNFOOT ROMAN FORT Near Eskdalemuir. This small fort was close to where the Roman road crossed the Esk.

RISPAIN CAMP South-west of Whithorn, A746, behind Rispain farm. Once believed to be a Roman camp and later a medieval site, radio-carbon dating has proved that this was a defended homestead of about 60BC. A surrounding ditch, with earth banks on either side and an entrance bridge of solid ground, is the most impressive feature.

TRUSTY'S HILL FORT AND SYMBOL STONE Gatehouse-of-Fleet, by the footpath to Anwoth Chuch. An oval summit fortified by ramparts, once timber-laced. Vitrification of the stone indicates that it may have been burnt at some time. It is remarkable in having the only Pictish symbols in Galloway cut on a rock by the entrance passage. The Picts lived in North East Scotland and it is possible that these symbols may have been carved to record a successful foray far from home. The name Trusty's Hill may possibly be associated with a Celtic Tristan.

TYNRON DOON FORT North-east of Moniave. The fort stands above the road from A702 to Tynron village. Occupying the summit of a hill at 289m in height, the fort has a magnificent site, easily defended, and is a conspicuous object in the landscape. Much of the hillside is so steep that it needs no further defence, but to the west and the south-west bold ramparts of earth and splintered rock tower over their intervening ditches, the lowest trench having been largely cut into rock. The interior formerly contained a number of circular dwellings. The outstanding position also attracted later generations and a C16th tower house once stood in one corner.

This region contains the earliest Christian memorials in Scotland and great abbeys built during the Middle Ages. After the Reformation the area became staunchly Protestant and many Covenanters suffered for their faith until Presbyterianism became the accepted form of worship for the Church of Scotland. Churchyards are often worth a visit as many contain interesting or elaborate monuments.

BUITTLE OLD PARISH CHURCH South-east of Castle Douglas, off A745. Now roofless, this parish church was built in the C13th and C14th, and in use until 1819.

CHAPEL FINIAN North-west of Port William, A747. The foundations of a small C10th or C11th chapel, named after an Irish saint educated at Whithorn. Possibly a landing place for pilgrims from Ireland to Whithorn.

CRUGGLETON CHURCH East of Whithorn off B7063. Parking restricted. Rebuilt in 1890 from the ruins of a small Romanesque church.

DALBEATTIE, ST. PETER'S CHURCH North-west of town centre. The oldest church in Dalbeattie, built in the growing town in 1814. A bequest from a member of the Maxwell family enabled the Roman Catholic faith to be re-established here after the Reformation

DUMFRIES, ST. MICHAEL'S CHURCH South of town centre. A large Georgian Hall church with a spire. The churchyard contains the imposing mausoleum of Robert Burns and an obelisk marking the site of the Covenanters' tombs, some with lengthy inscriptions, and many other elaborate monuments.

DUNDRENNAN ABBEY South-east of Kirkcudbright, off A711. This magnificent abbey was founded abouyt 1142 as a daughter house of Rievaulx in Yorkshire, the first of the great Cistercian monasteries in Britain, and a reference to it in 1165 as 'the abbey which the brethren of Rievaulx built' may account for the sophistication of the workmanship in what was then a remote region. The scale becomes apparent as the visitor realises that the beautiful pillared and arched remains comprise only the transepts and chancel of a once enormous church which was itself only the central part of a whole complex of buildings serving not only monks but also the needs of a large number of lay brethren. The religious enthusiasm of the C12th which had founded it gradually waned and the buildings were already decaying before the Reformation.

DURRISDEER CHURCH North of Thornhill, Nithsdale. Signposted off the A702. Built in 1699, this unexpectedly grand parish church contains the remarkable baroque burial aisle of the Queensberry family of Drumlanrig Castle.

GLENLUCE ABBEY North of Glenluce. Signposted from A75. The abbey was founded by Roland Lord of Galloway in 119 1/2, as a daughter house of Dundrennan. Little remains of the church but the chapter house, where abbot and monks met to discuss the affairs of the abbey, still stands. Rebuilt in the C15th, it still has its stone vaulted roof, traceried windows and stone bench around the walls. The ground plan of the domestic buildings for monks and lay brethren is recognisable. Earthenware jointed pipes for the water supply are an interesting survival.

KIRKMADRINE EARLY CHRISTIAN STONES South of Sandhead (Rhins). Signposts from A716. The chapel was rebuilt in the C19th from medieval ruins here. In a glass-fronted porch are very early Christian monuments, including an incised stone from the C5th, recording in Latin the resting place of three bishops.

LINCLUDEN COLLEGIATE CHURCH North of Dumfries. Signposted from A76. The nunnery on the site was abolished when only four nuns remained in 1389, and Archibald Earl of Douglas was given permission to establish a college of secular priests. It was at the time the fashion among the nobility to endow such religious establishments, whose main duty was to fulfil the spiritual needs of the family and to celebrate masses for the souls of the founder and his heirs. It also provided a wealthy man with the opportunity to show off his wealth and prestige. The architect was John Morow, a master mason who had been born in Paris but who is known to have worked at Melrose. Even in its battered state Lincluden can be seen as a gem of medieval architecture, and the wealth of stone carving repays close study. Notable is the tomb of Princess Margaret, widow of the fourth Earl.

MERKLAND CROSS North-west of Gretna Green, 8km on the A74, beside a farm road in a field. A late medieval wayside cross, apparently a monolith, with a circular floriated head. It is not certain what it commemorates.

MONIAIVE A702. Just west of the town is the monument to James Renwick, the last of the Covenanters to be executed, February 1688. Covenanters, sometimes numbered in thousands, would gather together in the hills to hear their preachers at conventicle sites.

NITH BRIDGE CROSS SHAFT   Thornhill. S. of A702, west of the river bridge. An Anglian cross. The top is missing but the shaft is carved with winged beasts and decorative plaits.

PORTPATRICK OLD PARISH CHURCH The church, now ruined, is dated 1629. The conspicuous circular tower would have been both a belfry and a useful beacon for ships entering the harbour.

RUTHWELL CROSS   Inside Ruthwell Parish Church west of Annan. Key from modern house near B724. An outstanding example of Christian art from the early C8th, famous far beyond Scotland. The 5.2m high stone cross was first recorded in 1600, inside the church. Regarded as 'an idolatrous monument' in 1642 it was broken up and buried. In 1823, its unique value recognised, it was reassembled as completely as possible and later placed in the church in a sunken apse which enables one to appreciate it easily. The sides are carved with a continuous design of vines, birds and animals, the margins decorated with runic symbols. On one front a boldly carved figure of Christ stands in majesty, his feet on two beasts, with a surrounding Latin text. Panels carved on the reverse include the Annunciation, a blind man healed and Mary Magdalen at Christ's feet.

ST. NINIAN'S CAVE   South of Whithorn, signposted from A747. Car park at Kidsdale and 1.8km walk to cave. A partly collapsed cave associated by tradition with St. Ninian. Small crosses incised on rock date at least from the C8th and C9th. Carved stones from the C11th and earlier, recovered from the debris, are now in the Whithorn Museum.

ST. NINIAN'S CHAPEL, Isle of Whithorn South of Whithorn. Car park in village and footpath. Restored and partly rebuilt in 1898, this small building may occupy a site associated with St. Ninian but no early Christian remains have been found here.

SWEETHEART ABBEY   South of Dumfries. Signposted on A710. Devorguilla de Balliol was devoted to her husband John, the founder of Balliol College, Oxford, and after his death, to honour his memory, founded this abbey for Cistercian monks, already established at Dundrennan and Glenluce. Her husband's heart she kept always by her in a silver casket and it was buried with her in her tomb, whence the abbey gets its name. Built during the years of English and Scottish wars and several times damaged by storms, its workmanship is of uneven quality, but it remains a magnificent monument in its completeness and its warm red sandstone. Although roofless, the walls and traceried windows still stand, saved by local people from demolition in 1779. The associated domestic buildings for the monks were almost entirely removed.

TERREGLES CHURCH AND 'QUEIR' North-west of Dumfries. Restored in 1875, this small church is of interest in having been built by a Roman Catholic family in 1583, when the Reformation was in full swing.

WHITHORN PRIORY, MUSEUM AND EXCAVATIONS   South of Wigtown, A746. It was in the early C5th, after Roman rule had collapsed, that St. Ninian came to Whithorn. Here he built the first church recorded in Scotland, the Casa Candida, or White House. Its exact location has been a matter of dispute and excavations in progress hope to throw more light on this remote period of history, the so-called 'Dark Ages'. What is certain is that Whithorn was a centre of Christian learning and its fame spread far and wide. Throughout the ensuing centuries, with struggles for supremacy between Celts, Anglians and Norsemen, wars between Scotland and England and disputes around the Scottish throne itself, Whithorn still remained a venerated shrine. In the late C12th a Premonstratensian Priory was established and a new church built over and around an earlier Romanesque church. The shrine of St. Ninian continued to attract many pilgrims, including Mary Queen of Scots, until pilgrimages were prohibited in 1581.
THE WHITHORN MUSEUM contains a remarkable collection of very early Christian stones and crosses dating back to the C5th.
WHITHORN PRIORY itself, now in ruins, nevertheless gives the visitor a formidable impression of its medieval splendour. WHITHORN DIG is an exciting archaeological excavation, with an observation platform for visitors and guides to explain the work. AN AUDIO VISUAL DISPLAY tells the story of the Christian history of the area.
THE NORSEMAN'S HOUSE being constructed is an authentic re-creation of a Viking House.
A MEDIEVAL GATEHOUSE forms the entrance.

WIGTOWN MARTYRS' TOMB   In the churchyard on the east side of the town. A railed enclosure contain the tombstones, dating from 1685, of Covenanters executed for their faith, including two women who were tied to a stake and drowned by the rising sea. An obelisk was erected on Windyhill in 1858 and a stone post marks the spot, now dry land, of the drowning.

Dumfries Museums

Days and times of opening vary throughout the year. Before making a special journey, it is advisable to check opening times, particularly in winter.

DUMFRIES MUSEUM In an C18th converted windmill on top of Corbelly Hill, 300 metres from Whitesands car park. The largest museum in south-west Scotland. A collection of local and national importance reflecting the colourful social and natural history of the area. Here you can wonder at the fossil footprints of prehistoric animals, admire the birds of the Solway salt marshes, examine the tools and weapons of the earliest people and the stone carving of Scotland's first Christians, see the local textiles and crafts and the Victorian farm, shop and home. One large gallery is devoted to local history, covering crime, witchcraft and medicine, as well as burgh life and trade.

CAMERA OBSCURA On the top floor of Windmill Tower. Installed in 1836 when the building was converted to an observatory. A moving panoramic image of Dumfries and the surrounding countryside, as far as 50 miles radius on a clear day, is reflected by a mirror onto a tabletop screen in a darkened room. An exhibition in the room below explains how the camera obscura works and includes the history of the windmill and its conversion to an observatory, together with the 8 inch Gregorian telescope made especially for it by Thomas Morton of Kilmarnock.

THE GROUNDS Pleasantly laid out with terraced lawns and flower beds, include a statue of Sir Walter Scott's 'Old Mortality', Robert Paterson, a stonemason from Balmaclellan in Kirkcudbright who travelled the region making tombstones for the unmarked graves of Covenanting martyrs.

DUMFRIES ARCHIVE CENTRE Opposite Robert Burns House. Although only opened in the summer of 1987, the Centre was awarded the Research Prize of the Scottish Museum of the Year Award for 1988. The archives date back to the C15th and include court, council and treasurers' records, police, jail, and poorhouse books, papers from local families, firms and societies, giving a full picture of the life of the community through the centuries in all its many aspects.

DUMFRIES OLD BRIDGE HOUSE A short walk from the town centre across the C15th Devorguilla Bridge. This was once the toll house for the bridge and now contains Victorian and Edwardian period rooms, including a dentist's surgery, kitchens and a child's nursery. giving a very realistic impression of past life.

ROBERT BURNS CENTRE Dumfries is closely associated with Robert Burns, who spent the last years of his life in the town. A special section of this guide-book is devoted to Robert Burns in Dumfries, and includes details of the Centre, the House where he lived and other places connected with the poet.

OTHER DUMFRIES MUSEUMS

CRICHTON ROYAL MUSEUM In the prestigious Crichton Royal Hospital, founded in 1839, this museum celebrates 150 years of medicine in the area. A former operating theatre, past records and publications are on display. together with examples of patients' art from early days to 1961. A specialist library is available for serious students. Garden and tea-room. Open afternoons, Thursday, Friday and Saturday.

DUMFRIES AND GALLOWAY AVIATION MUSEUM Heathall Industrial Estate. At a former RAF airfield control tower, the museum has aircraft, engines, flying clothing and all kinds of aviation artifacts and memorabilia. Run entirely by dedicated enthusiasts. Open Sundays in season only.

GRACEFIELD ARTS CENTRE Edinburgh Road. This public Art Gallery, the only one in south-west Scotland, was opened in 1951. It has a fine collection of C20th Scottish painting, and also puts on a series of different exhibitions of work by contemporary artists throughout the year. These may be devoted to the work of a single individual or of a group of artists. Photography is included. A number of studios and a dark room are also available for use, and there is a pottery workshop and a small sculpture area. A Meetings Room and a cafe/bar make the Centre a pleasant and friendly place and local societies such as the Fine Arts Society, the Embroiderers' Guild and the Camera Club meet regularly to discuss and exhibit their work. Visitors to the Dumfries region will find this a most interesting place to see a whole range of work being done in Scotland today.

DUMFRIES PRIORY CHRISTIAN HERITAGE MUSEUM Maxwell Street. As well as visiting the monastic ruins of Dumfries and Galloway, find out about the lives of the people who dwelt in them. This museum traces the history of monasticism in south-west Scotland, and includes a miniature 'son et lumiere'. There is also a display of embroidered Church vestments. There is a coffee room. Open from Easter to the end of September (winter by appointment).

DUMFRIES' MUSEUMS

Visit Dumfries' Museums and discover the story of the town and its surroundings. See how the townfolk lived in times past and learn about Robert Burns and the time he spent there. There's something to interest everyone from first time visitor to native 'Doonhamer'.

DUMFRIES MUSEUM, Church Street
10 – 1, 2 – 5 Mon – Sat, 2 – 5 Sun
Closed Sun & Mon Oct – March
Admission Free

CAMERA OBSCURA,
Dumfries Museum
10 – 1, 2 – 5 Mon – Sat, 2 – 5 Sun
Closed Oct – March
Admission 50p (adults) 25p (concessions)

OLD BRIDGE HOUSE, Mill Road
10 – 1, 2 – 5 Mon – Sat, 2 – 5 Sun
Closed Oct – March
Admission Free

BURNS HOUSE, Burns Street
10 – 1, 2 – 5 Mon – Sat 2 – 5 Sun
Closed Sun & Mon Oct – March
Admission 50p (adults) 25p (concessions)

How to get there

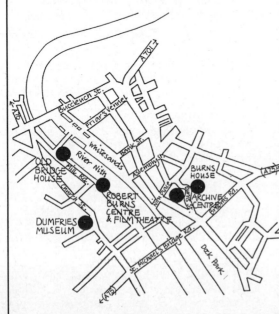

ROBERT BURNS CENTRE, Mill Road
10 – 8 Mon – Sat, 2 – 5 Sun (April –Sept)
10 – 1 , 2 – 5 Tue – Sat (Oct – March)
Admission Free
Audio Visual 50p (adults)
25p (concessions)

FILM THEATRE, Robert Burns Centre
Open Tues – Sat,
Films start 8.00pm Aril – Sept
7.30pm Oct – March
Admission Adults £2.00
Concessions £1.50 'Family' ticket
(2 adults, 2 children) £5.00

DUMFRIES ARCHIVE CENTRE,
Burns Street
11 – 1, 2 – 5 Tues, Wed, Friday
6pm – 9pm Thursday
Admission Free

SAVER TICKET
A Museum's Saver Ticket costing £1.00 and valid for one week gives admission to the Camera Obscura, the audio-visual theatre at the Robert Burns Centre and Burns House, and can be purchased at any of these premises.

Museums in Dumfries are detailed on a separate page.

Remember that days and times of opening vary greatly, some places being open daily in July and August but closed entirely in winter, and check before undertaking a special journey.

CREETOWN GEM ROCK MUSEUM See details under 'Three Unusual Museums'.

DEER MUSEUM, CLATTERINGSHAWS See details under 'Natural History'.

ECCLEFECHAN, CARLYLE'S BIRTHPLACE See details under 'National Trust for Scotland Properties'.

GLENLUCE MOTOR MUSEUM North of Glenluce. Vintage and classic cars, motor bikes and motoring memorabilia, displayed with period costumes. Fire engine for children. Old fashioned garage with restoration work on show.

GRETNA GREEN, THE OLD BLACKSMITH'S SHOP VISITOR CENTRE See under 'Three Unusual Museums'.

GRETNA HALL MARRIAGE ROOM AND BLACKSMITH'S SHOP At Gretna Hall Hotel. The original marriage house where marriages were performed over the anvil, symbolic of joining twp people together as the blacksmith joins metal. Visitors can reaffirm their vows in this romantic setting.

GRETNA OLD TOLL BAR When a turnpike road was built over the River Sark in 1820, this became the first house over the border, where the toll keepers performed over 10,000 marriages.

KIRKCUDBRIGHT, BROUGHTON HOUSE, High Street. An C18th house with fine furniture, the home of E.A. Hornel (1864-1933), one of the leaders of the Glasgow school of painting, with exhibitions and mementoes. Children are made welcome. An antiquarian library with notable Burns items is available on special request. See also 'Gardens of the Area'.

KIRKCUDBRIGHT, STEWARTRY MUSEUM, St. Mary's Street. This is an important museum of the history, domestic life, agriculture and natural history of this area, and includes the work of local artists. A visit here will increase your understanding and enjoyment of the region.

KIRKPATRICK DURHAM, MOONSTONE MINIATURES A fascinating display of miniatures and furnished houses and shops, to one twelfth scale. Check opening times.

LANGHOLM, THE CRAIGCLEUGH COLLECTION West of Langholm on B709. In a fine Scottish Baronial style mansion, the Scottish Explorers' Museum, with an incredible and fascinating display of items from all over the world, tribal masks, silk paintings, American Indian stone animals, Japanese ivories, Chinese jade and numerous other curiosities.

MOFFAT MUSEUM In an old bakehouse, the story of Moffat, from the early days of the border raiders, through the fierce persecution of the Covenanters, to the prosperous days when Moffat was one of only two spa towns in Scotland.

NEW GALLOWAY, GALLOWAY FARM MUSEUM See details under 'Farming'.

NEW ABBEY CORN MILL See under 'Industry'.

NEW ABBEY, SHAMBELLIE HOUSE MUSEUM OF COSTUME (National Museums of Scotland) On A710. In a Scottish Baronial style house, a delightful display of clothes, ball-gowns and fashion accessories, drawn mainly from the huge collection made by Charles Stewart of Shambellie, and renewed annually, which are shown in a natural manner in the fine rooms.

NEWTON STEWART MUSEUM York Road. Run entirely by local people, an outstanding collection of clothes, including court dresses and 1920s items, shawls and lace, as well as old domestic and farming implements. A fascinating reminder of a disappearing world.

PORTPATRICK, LITTLE WHEELS See details under 'Three Unusual Museums'.

RUTHWELL, SAVINGS BANK MUSEUM In the building where the Rev. Henry Duncan opened the Ruthwell Parish Bank in 1810. You can see the three- lock money box and the early documents, and follow the development of his idea into the Trustee Savings Banks of today.

SANQUHAR TOLBOOTH VISITOR CENTRE Famous for the Covenanters' declarations, with the oldest post office in Britain, with stirring tales of its former castle, and once a coal mining centre, Sanquhar has a long and enthralling story to tell.

SKYREBURN AQUARIUM South-west of Gatehouse-of-Fleet. This could, perhaps, be considered a museum of live fish. See chapter on 'Natural History and Nature Reserves'.

STRANRAER MUSEUM Displays of natural history, archaeology and local history , as well as work by local artists. Being refurbished.

WANLOCKHEAD, MUSEUM OF SCOTTISH LEAD MINING An extensive and absorbing indoor and open air museum. See details under ' Industry'.

WHITHORN PRIORY, MUSEUM AND EXCAVATIONS The earliest Christian foundation in Scotland. See details under 'Christian Sites and Abbeys'.

Three Unusual Museums

CREETOWN THE CREETOWN GEM ROCK MUSEUM Signposted on A75 between Newton Stewart and Gatehouse-of-Fleet. An amazing display of minerals, gem stones and fossils collected from all over the world by the Stephenson family. The collection was started by Maurice Stephenson over fifty years ago and is now very comprehensive, with many thousands of exhibits, making up what must be the largest private collection of its kind on permanent display to the public in Britain. The overall theme is to show off the wonderful world of minerals and gemstones, and to explain the art of gem cutting. On display are not only minerals, but also untouched gem quality crystals, and intricately polished gemstones, carved gem figurines, and objets d'art, as well as fossils and stone age artifacts, all of which make the museum a unique and amazingly beautiful place to visit.

A huge amethyst with beautiful dark crystals greets the visitor at the entrance, for one of the unusual things about the museum is the remarkable size of the specimens. Another display very popular with visitors is the fluorescent mineral exhibit. The minerals are at first automatically illuminated by ordinary white light, to reveal some interesting but not very colourful specimens, and then, as if by magic, the whole scene is transformed into a display of unbelievable fluorescent colour, an effect breath-taking for the visitor in the midst of it. There is so much to be seen that it is impossible to take it all in on a single visit and it is these wonderful effects and the overall atmosphere which make the first impression on the visitor.

THE WORKSHOP, where many of the gem and mineral gifts and jewellery articles are made, is open to visitors and here they can watch the fascinating art of gem-cutting, done to show the stone to its best advantage. Many of the items made here are available in the gift shop. There is also an excellent tearoom/restaurant, open throughout the day. The Museum is open from March 1st to the end of December, every day from 9.30 am to 6.0 pm.

GRETNA GREEN - THE OLD BLACKSMITH'S SHOP AND VISITOR CENTRE On A6071 between Longtown and Gretna, in former days the coaching road from Longtown and Carlisle. This village on the border between Scotland and England has become famous because of its romantic association with runaway marriages. These marriages were brought about by the difference in marriage laws between the two countries. In Scotland anyone could be married without parental consent at the age of sixteen, by any responsible person, such as a blacksmith, simply by declaring themselves before two witnesses.

The first noted 'Gretna Priest' was Joseph Paisley in 1750 (a twenty stone whisky imbiber) and the line continued uninterrupted util 1940, when Richard Rennison performed the last legal marriage in the Old Blacksmith's Shop (one of 5,147). This old building, made of 'clay daubin' and built in 1730, captured the imagination of the world and is now an interesting Museum and Visitor Centre. Here you can see the famous marriage anvil and also a magnificent collection of horse-drawn coaches and carriages, including a state landau. Visitors, greeted by a bagpipe player, are well catered for, with a large self-service restaurant, and a shop with tweed, tartans and souvenirs of Scotland. The Museum and Visitor Centre are open daily all year, the hours varying with the season and being somewhat reduced in the winter months.

PORTPATRICK 'LITTLE WHEELS' Hill Street. Signposted. It is a long time now since trains puffed up the line from Stranraer, over the crossing at Colvin and through the curved cutting into Portpatrick station. Whether they will ever come back is in the crystal ball of the future - yet they are already back in one form. In a quiet street in Portpatrick, 125 Intercity trains are speeding through tunnels and across viaducts; shunting engines fuss on side tracks; historic engines of the great days of LMS and GWR haul pullman, sleeper and passenger coaches in the great liveries of yesteryear.

All around are display cases of other engines and trains; cars and trucks and lorries; ships; industrial engines; horse drawn coaches and bright tin-plate toys in a Lilliput wonderworld of memorabilia and models. The display has been planned in a manner which sets off everything to its best advantage, and it includes many unusual models and toys from far-off countries. 'Little Wheels' is, of course, still being added to, so that it is no static museum display or dust-gathering exhibition. It is moving and growing continuously and those who come to see it will find something that captures their attention time after time.

This is a unique and fascinating display which will be enjoyed by all ages from the young to the old. It is open from Easter to the end of October every day except Friday, and in the peak holiday season of July and August it is open every day including Friday.

AMISFIELD Small village with nearby privately owned C16th Amisfield Tower.

ANNAN See entry on Contents page.

ANWOTH There was a church here from at least the C12th. The Presbyterian scholar Samuel Rutherford was minister in Anwoth from 1627 to 1639, and is commemorated by an obelisk.

ARDWELL A village on the shores of Luce Bay, with a former mill. There is a large picnic area. Ardwell House is a C17th house with fine gardens open to the public.

AUCHENCAIRN Once an iron and barytes mining centre and haunt of smugglers, now a most attractive seaside village. In the bay is Hestan Island with a lighthouse.

AULDGIRTH The Nith here runs through a gorge. Carlyle's father, a stone-mason, helped to build the bridge. Nearby is Dalswinton Loch where a steamship was tried out in 1788. Burns farmed close by at Ellisland.

BALMACLELLAN An attractive hillside village. Celtic relics have been found in the area,. This was once a centre of the Covenanters' faith. There is a statue to Robert Paterson, Scott's 'Old Mortality'.

BARGRENNAN Close to Glentrool and beautiful country. Nearby ancient cairns have been found.

BEATTOCK Just off the main A74 road to Glasgow. Ideal for Lowther Hills. The Southern Upland Way passes here. Nearby is a waterfall on the Annan river. Beattock summit is the highest point at 1,029ft (315m) on the route to the Clyde valley and was a notable uphill pull in the days of steam trains.

BEESWING An interesting C19th planned estate village. In a good area for bird watching.

BIRKHILL At the top of a pass in the Lowther Hills. Once a refuge for Covenanters.

BLADNOCH There is a creamery here and also the Bladnoch Distillery which can be visited.

BORGUE The Borgue Academy was founded in 1802 by Thomas Rainy who had made a fortune in Dominica. It acquired an excellent reputation.

BROW Once a small watering place by the Solway Firth, it was here that Burns came in the hope of curing his final illness.

CAERLAVEROCK Close to the Solway Firth and the National Nature Reserve where thousands of birds winter, and to the great C13th fortress of Caerlaverock Castle.

CAIRNRYAN An attractive village of white-painted houses, once the homes of oyster fishermen, and a fine Queen Anne house. Used as a military port during the last War, and now a ferry trminal from Larne in Northern Ireland.

CANONBIE At the southern end of Eskdale near the junction with Liddesdale, once the lawless 'Debatable Lands, Johnnie Armstrong's Hollows Tower is nearby. There is an old coaching inn in the pleasant village.

CARSETHORN An unspoiled village with a harbour which once took transatlantic trade.

CARSPHAIRN An attractive village with a white painted church. Nearby lead mines employed 300 people in the C19th.

CASTLE DOUGLAS See entry on Contents page.

CLARENCEFIELD Close to the Solway Firth. Nearby is Comlongon Castle.

CLOSEBURN Burns visited the nearby Closeburn Tower (not open). From here roads lead into the hills. The Crichope Linn ravine is described by Scott in 'Old Mortality'.

COLVEND Popular holiday village. Golf course.

CREETOWN On one of the most beautiful coast roads in Southern Scotland. Once a busy port from which granite, quarried nearby, was shipped. The old harbour and waterfront has some good C18th and early C19th houses. A clock tower commemorates Queen Victoria's diamond jubilee. The old school is now the Creetown Gem Rock Museum.

CROCKETFORD Founded by a religious sect led by the eccentric Mother Buchan in the C18th.

CROSSMICHAEL Very good bird watching area.

CRUGGLETON A medieval parish with a Norman church (restored in 1892). Cruggleton, or Rigg, Bay was used for testing the 'Mulberry Harbours', used in the invasion of Normandy.

CUMMERTREES The notorious tides of the Solway Firth can be seen from here. The district is described in Scott's 'Redgauntlet'. Robert Bruce is said to have founded the church.

DALBEATTIE See entry on Contents page.

DALRY Properly St. John's Town of Dalry. On the ancient Pilgrims Way to Whithorn. King James IV stopped here in 1507. To the north east is Lochinvar, famous in a ballad.

DORNOCK Near the Solway Firth, with remnants of a stone circle and two ancient towers nearby.

DOUGLAS HALL A small holiday resort by the Solway Firth, on a most attractive stretch of coast overlooking Sandyhills Bay. There are two natural rock arches nearby.

DRUMMORE coal and lime were once imported and farm produce exported. A large mill and store still stand above the harbour.

DUMFRIES See entry on Contents page.

DUNDRENNAN An attractive village, built partly of stones taken from the Abbey in the past. The great abbey dates from 1142, and from here Mary Queen of Scots left Scotland for ever.

DUNRAGIT On high ground to the north of the A75 and overlooking Luce Bay. In recent years an interesting new rock and bog garden has been created at Glenwhan and can be visited.

DUNSCORE In the fertile farming area around the Cairn Water. Here Burns set up a library. To the north is the ruined tower of Lag, once home of the hated Grierson of Lag.

DURISDEER The church, dating from 1699 contains the elaborate memorial aisle of the Queensberry family of nearby Drumlanrig. Well Path is an ancient track, possibly originally Roman, and a small Roman fortlet is nearby.

ECCLEFECHAN Famous as the birthplace of Thomas Carlyle, called Entepfuhl in his book 'Sartor Resartus'. Carlyle's uncle and father were master masons and the house with its arched entrance is typical of a prosperous artisan's home of the period. Carlyle lived in London but wished to be buried in his home village.

ELRIG This was once a thriving place with the largest grain mills in the Machars region. Gavin Maxwell's book 'The House of Elrig' is about his childhood in the region.

ESKDALEMUIR At the north end of the remote and peaceful Eskdale. Tibetan refugees chose this locality to build the only Tibetan monastery in Britain. It is also the site of an observatory which monitors seismic activity and of a meteorological station, its name being familiar to many in national weather forecasts.

EWES CHURCH North of Langholm. The church bell hangs in the fork of a tree.

GARLIESTON Laid out in a crescent round the bay by Lord Garlies about 1760, with ship building and a corn mill as local industries. The gardens of Galloway House are nearby.

GATEHOUSE-OF-FLEET A planned town laid out on a grid pattern by James Murray of Broughton with cotton mills and a brewery close to the water which provided the power to drive the machinery. A canal was cut by Irish labourers (Murray had estates in Ireland) to improve the harbour. There are a number of C18th and C19th workers cottages, with larger two storey houses for the artisans and craftsmen.

GLENCAPLE Once a busy port near Dumfries with quays from which ships sailed to America and the West Indies, and well known to Burns in his duties as an excise officer.

GLENLUCE Long an important crossing point on the Water of Luce. The ruins of Glenluce Abbey are nearby, and so is the commanding Castle of Park tower. Golf course.

GLENTROOL Originally built to house forestry workers, but now a mixture of houses, some privately owned.

GRETNA AND GRETNA GREEN See entry on Contents page.

HIGHTAE In farming country by the river Annan, with a fine house, Rammerscales, nearby.

HODDOM BRIDGE An ancient Christian foundation dating back to the C6th. A crossing point over the Annan once defended by Hoddom Castle. A visitors' lodge illustrates the running of the farming and forestry Hoddom Estate.

INNERMESSAN On the eastern shores of Loch Ryan, the settlement can be traced back to at least medieval times. The C16th Craigcaffie tower house is nearby.

IRONGRAY A pleasant village by the Cluden Water. In the churchyard is a memorial erected by Scott to Helen Walker. On nearby Skeogh Hill in 1678 3,000 Covenanters took communion, an place now marked by an obelisk. There is also an inscribed tombstone to a Covenanter.

ISLE OF WHITHORN On a rocky shore, sheltered by a headland, this was a busy C19th port, which also employed a number of men in ship-building. Believed to be a landing place for St. Ninian, and revered since the C4th, it was for long a place of pilgrimage and the small ruined chapel dates from the C13th.

JOHNSTONE BRIDGE North of Lockerbie, this has long been a major crossing point over the Annan river and a place from which to explore this beautiful valley.

KEIR A small place famous in the history of transport, for it was here that Kirkpatrick Macmillan invented the first bicycle. His original machine is in the Science Museum in London but there is a copy in the Dumfries Museum. A plaque commemorates his achievement.

KELLS CHURCHYARD On the northern outskirts of New Galloway, with remarkable tombstones, three depicting Adam and Eve, and including a headstone to a gamekeeper, showing his dog, gun, powder-flask, fishing rod and partridge-like bird.

KIPPFORD This was a busy ship-building and fishing centre at the beginning of the C19th. From the 1870s onwards it developed as a resort for sea-bathing and leisure. Now a popular yachting place with an annual regatta.

KIRKANDREWS The old churchyard is a site which may well have had links with the early Celtic Church and Iona. Sailing ships used to be able to moor in the bay. A remarkable collection of farm buildings with a castellated tower and an arched entrance were built by James Brown, a Manchester businessman, early this century.

KIRKBEAN The attractive church with its dome-shaped tower was built in 1835. The font was presented in 1945 by the American Navy in honour of John Paul Jones, born nearby at Arbigland. This garden can be visited.

KIRKCOLM The attractive terraces of single and two storey cottages, painted white, were originally homes of fishermen. To the north-west is Corsewall Point with a lighthouse designed by Robert Stephenson in 1815.

KIRKCONNEL This was a former mining village and has a memorial to all the miners killed over the years in the former mines. Covenanters met in the surrounding hills.

KIRKCOWAN Near the village the old weaving sheds for wool, an old chimney and an old waulk mill, now all disused, indicate the past industrial importance of the area. The church still retains its outside stair.

KIRKCUDBRIGHT See entry on Contents page.

KIRKGUNZEON There was probably a settlement here by the C12th. Attractive single and two storey painted houses line the road. The churchyard has remarkably tall monuments, including a steeple tomb.

KIRKINNER The old church was probably on an early Christian site and there is an Anglian cross in the churchyard. The layout is typical of a C19th strip village along the road.

KIRKLAND A small place close to Maxwelton House, the home of Bonnie Annie Laurie, now restored and with fine gardens open to the public.

KIRKMAIDEN In Scotland's most southerly point. Burns wrote 'Frae Maidenkirk to Johnny Groats'. This was an important holy place in early Christian and Medieval times, with a number of chapels and holy wells in the vicinity.

KIRKPATRICK DURHAM A good example of a planned village laid out with four intersecting streets and single storey cottages, founded in 1783 by the minister and landowner, Dr. David Lamont (later Moderator of the General Assembly), with cotton and woollen manufactures, inns and a racecourse.

KIRKPATRICK FLEMING To the west is a cave reputed to have been a hiding place of Bruce.

KIRTLEBRIDGE In an area once renowned for lawlessness, with several old towers in the vicinity. Nearby is the famous C15th Merkland Cross. At the ruined Kirkconnell Church is the grave of 'Fair Helen of Kirkconnell Lee'.

LANGHOLM See entry on Contents page.

LAURIESTON There is a memorial here to S.R. Crockett, who wrote 'The Raiders', the name given to a Forestry Drive off A712.

LESWALT There is a 60ft high monument to Sir Andrew Agnew of Lochnaw who laid out Aldouran Glen with exotic trees, rare plants and paths. Nearby is the C15 Lochnaw Castle. Rhododendrons are a feature of the landscape here.

LOCHANS A typical Galloway village south of Stranraer. An old tower house stands nearby.

LOCHFOOT Small village on the shores of Lochrutton Loch. An old tower is nearby.

LOCHMABEN The town grew up around a de Brus motte and bailey castle, it being first mentioned in 1173. It became a Royal Burgh about 1440. Lochmaben Castle was an important strategic point, taken and retaken several times. Castle Loch and Hightae Loch are nature reserves. Fishing and golf available.

LOCKERBIE Now sadly world-famous after the aircraft disaster. A market town for Annandale with a Lamb Fair dating from the C17th, and Common Ridings recalling earlier turbulent times. Burnswark Fort is nearby. A good central point from which to explore, both hills and coast being easily reached. With hotels, caravan and camping sites and a golf course.

MENNOCK At the foot of the Lowther Hills. From here a road leads up the Mennock Pass.

MOFFAT See entry on Contents page.

MONIAIVE Three streams meet by this most attractive village of painted cottages. The village cross dates from 1638. This was a centre for the Covenanters and to the west is a monument to James Renwick, the last to be executed. Nearby is the Iron Age Tynron Doon Fort on a spectacular hilltop.

MONREITH Set round a bay, formerly a haunt of smugglers, now a popular holiday village. A memorial to Gavin Maxwell, of the Elrig and Monreith family, is on a headland.

MOUSWALD A small village with a tall C18th windmill tower still standing.

NEW ABBEY In an attractive wooded situation by the Pow Burn. Famous for the ruins of Sweetheart Abbey. Additional attractions include the New Abbey Corn Mill and the Shambellie House Museum of Costume.

NEW BRIDGE The bridge crosses the Cluden Water. Nearby is the 'Twelve Apostles" stone circle.

NEW GALLOWAY This is the smallest Royal Burgh in Scotland, established by Viscount Kenmure in 1633. The fine granite bridge was built by Rennie. This district needed 10,000 Highland troops to subdue the Covenanters. Now a good holiday centre with golf, fishing and watersports in the vicinity, and also the RSPB Ken-Dee Reserve.

NEW LUCE By the meeting of the Main Water and Cross Water of Luce, an attractive village with its old cottages restored.

NEWTON STEWART See entry on Contents page.

PALNACKIE Once the main port on the Urr estuary, exporting millstones as far back as the C17th, and extremely busy in the C19th when it imported slates, coal and timber and exported the produce of this rich agricultural district. The home of the celebrated World Flounder Tramping Championship. There are a number of craft workshops in the area.

PALNURE Once a busy harbour, exporting timber, grain and lead from local mines. The attractive Bargaly Glen is nearby.

PENPONT On the Scar Water. By the ancient pilgrims' track from Edinburgh to Whithorn, taken by James IV on occasion. Birthplace of the African explorer Joseph Thomson, who gave his name to Thomson's gazelle.

PORT LOGAN A small planned village laid out in 1818 by Colonel Andrew McDowall with a row of houses lining the bay and another row of cottages further up the hill. The port proved too exposed for the Irish ferry trade he had hoped for, but the picturesque lighthouse still stands. The famous Logan Fish Pond is close to the bay and Logan Botanic Gardens nearby.

PORTPATRICK See entry on Contents page.

PORT WILLIAM Founded by Sir William Maxwell in 1775, with fishing and ship-building trades, but also a noted place for smugglers, where two armed luggers with 50 men apiece were once discovered about to land their goods. Now a popular holiday place with a slipway for boats.

POWFOOT Where the Pow Water joins the Solway Firth, a former fishing village, now a holiday resort with camping and caravanning facilities and an 18-hole golf course.

RINGFORD A monument here recalls the murder of five Covenanters by Grierson of Lag.

ROCKCLIFFE A very popular holiday area, also favoured by the Victorians, with yachts in summer, walks along the Jubilee Path and Muckle Lands, the Mote of Mark Hill Fort, and Rough Island Bird Sanctuary.

RUTHWELL Known everywhere for the celebrated Ruthwell Cross, now in a specially built apse in the church. A famous Dark Ages relic, with carved figures and inscriptions in Latin and Runic, it was thrown down as a 'monstrous idol' in 1642 but restored in 1823. The Trustee Savings Bank Museum is here, where the first parish bank was founded.

ST. ANNS On the Kinnel Water. The bridge dates from 1800. The pretty Raehills Glen is nearby.

SANDHEAD Once a place used for landing lime and coal. Today a popular holiday resort, with miles of golden sandy beaches by Luce Bay, camping and caravans. Within a short distance is Kirkmadrine Church, which has some of the earliest Christian monuments in Scotland.

SANDYHILLS Seaside village with a large sandy beach intersected by a river. Very popular.

SANQUHAR There are remains of an ancient castle here. The town became a Royal Burgh in 1598. The staple industry was coal-mining, where in the early days the miners and their families lived in bondage, unable to move or change their occupation, working under terrible conditions. The last mine closed in the 1960s. The town is famous for the Covenanters Richard Cameron and James Renwick and their defiance of the king. The Post Office is the oldest in Britain, dated 1763. The fine Georgian Tolbooth of 1735 is now a visitor centre.

SHAWHEAD To the north-west, by Glenkiln Loch, are sculptures by Henry Moore and Rodin. These are on private ground and may not be approached but are visible from the road.

SOUTHERNESS A pleasant resort with caravans, camping and an 18-hole golf course. The disused lighthouse is one of the oldest in Scotland. The famous Arbigland Gardens are close by.

SOUTHWICK There was a Gilbert de Suthayk in 1180. Known to the Victorians as the 'Scottish Riviera', the area is attractive with woodland, the Mersehead Sands and the unusual geological features of the Needles Eye and Lot's Wife. The parish contains the village of Caulkerbush.

SPRINGFIELD A village founded in 1791 as a centre for weaving.

STRANRAER See entry on Contents page.

TERREGLES The church is known for its choir, dating from 1583, and important monuments.

THORNHILL Pleasant town with a wide tree-lined main street, and a tall column surmounted by the Queensberry emblem of a winged horse. Near the river is the shaft of an Anglian Cross. A cross in nearby Dalgarnock churchyard commemorates 57 martyred Covenanters.

TINWALD An ancient meeting place. Tinwald Downs was formerly an air-base.

TONGLAND Dominated by the hydro-electric power station, with a fish-pass for salmon. The bridge was designed by Telford.

TWYNHOLM Settlement here can be traced back to Iron Age times. In the C18th and C19th, it was a busy place with a cornmill, sawmills and blanket and tweed weaving.

TYNRON In the hilly country which was a refuge for Covenanters. Tynron Doon Iron Age fort stands on a commanding hilltop.

WANLOCKHEAD Scotland's highest village. Originally, situated in this wild and beautiful country because of the mineral wealth in the hills. Known from early times and extensively developed in the C18th and C19th. Site of the Museum of lead mining, with mine, machinery and cottages on show.

WESTERKIRK A remote village in Eskdale with a monument to Thomas Telford who was born here.

WHITHORN The place where St. Ninian founded the first Christian church in Scotland.

WIGTOWN See entry on Contents page.

Advertiser's Index